THE VENTURI SYSTEM

Books by Ken Venturi

KEN VENTURI'S STROKE SAVERS • 1986
(with Don Wade)

THE VENTURI SYSTEM • 1983
(with Al Barkow)

THE VENTURI ANALYSIS • 1981
(with Al Barkow)

THE VENTURI SYSTEM

With Special Material on Shotmaking
for the Advanced Golfer
by

KEN VENTURI
with Al Barkow

Illustrations by Dom Lupo
Special Editorial Consultant, Desmond Tolhurst

ATHENEUM   NEW YORK

Atheneum
Macmillan Publishing Company
866 Third Avenue, New York, N.Y. 10022
Collier Macmillan Canada, Inc.

Library of Congress Cataloging-in-Publication Data

Venturi, Ken.
The Venturi system.

1. Golf   I. Barkow, Al.   II. Lupo, Dom.   III. Title.
GV965.V453   1983   796.352′3   83-45088
ISBN 0-689-11414-1

Macmillan books are available at special discounts for bulk purchases
for sales promotions, premiums, fund-raising, or educational use.
For details, contact:

Special Sales Director
Macmillan Publishing Company
866 Third Avenue
New York, N.Y. 10022

10 9 8 7 6 5 4 3

Printed in the United States of America

This book is dedicated to Byron Nelson.
He gave me his time, effort, and knowledge,
for which I am forever indebted.
I shall always treasure
his loyalty and friendship.

KEN VENTURI

FOREWORD

On one of his CBS golf telecasts, Ken Venturi was giving a tip on how to play a very difficult shot. The ball was beside a green, but although there was a clear path to the putting surface, it was up against a tree in such a way that Ken could not swing in anything like the conventional manner. The tree was where he, as a right-handed golfer, would ordinarily stand at the ball. Ken's tip was: Stand on the left-hander's side with your back to the hole, hold the club in your right hand and set the clubhead up on its toe with its face aimed at the green, then swing like someone flicking a bit of trash behind them. Ken did all this, made the swing, hit the ball per- fectly, *and 2 inches from the hole some 100 feet away.* A phenomenal shot! Ken fell against the tree with an amazed smile. As they say in television, it was a "one-take."

Ken Venturi has an uncanny knack for this kind of thing. That shot for television was but one outrageous example. While working on this book, Venturi would demonstrate what he meant about certain shots, and would repeatedly pull them off exactly as he said he would.

"Here, Al, I'll hit a pitch shot that will take two bounces and stop." It took two bounces and stopped.

"Now a little four-foot draw, three bounces, stop." It drew 4 feet, took three bounces, and stopped. I kid you not. He did this kind of thing maybe 90 percent of the time.

I was regularly awed by this display, but, keeping my wits about me and with our book in mind, I finally asked Ken how he could do such things. His response gets to one of the overriding themes running through this book. He said he can hit such shots because he is not thinking about the ball, only about the shot.

That is to say, if we focus our attention so completely on the ball itself – admittedly not an unnatural thing to do – the ball in a sense comes to dominate us. We lose sight of the fact that it is, in fact, an inert, mindless object that will do anything we command it to do. That "commanding" is the swing we apply to it.

Ken illustrates the point this way: "The golf swing is a backswing and a follow-through, with the golf ball something that the club passes through. A good player corrects his game by being conscious of his swing. A poor player remains a poor player because he is conscious only of the ball.

"What I am trying to produce with this book is a simplification of a complex action. Rather than trying to produce a ball motion, I am trying to make a golf club swing. And here's an important thought in that respect. If you could have a golfer start his swing without a ball there, then suddenly inject the ball in front of the club in the middle of his downswing, he would probably hit the best shot of his life."

Allied to this notion of eliminating ball-consciousness – or its intimidation factor – is another theme running through The Venturi System, namely, that we all swing much too hard at the ball, perhaps because we see it as an enemy trying to destroy us and so go after it hammer and claw. Ken advocates, in essence, what might be called Three-Quarter Golf. That is not to say you consciously swing the club with a backswing shortened by a quarter, although this might result. Rather, in thinking "Do not force it," you develop a tempo and a degree of club control that produces more solidly hit balls than you ever thought you had in you. What is more, this approach seems to satisfy that great need so many golfers have for distance. The fascinating thing about Three-Quarter Golf is the power the shots have.

I can tell you one thing: Ken Venturi means — totally believes in — what he says in this book. He told me when we first began, "You can ask me about a piece of technique today, and again three months later, and again if you like three years later, and each time the answer will be the same."

Not that I didn't believe him, but it so happened that in the course of gathering the material for this book, some questions about technique were repeated. Later, when I put all my notes together in categories, I found what amounted to carbon copies of Ken's original answers.

AL BARKOW
Upper Montclair, N.J.

CONTENTS

"You cannot correct a fault with a fault. That is why I do not talk about theories, but about fundamentals, and why I always go back to fundamentals."

—Ken Venturi

PROLOGUE

PLAYING THE ANGLES

There are many working parts and movements in a golf swing, so it can become a complex piece of business—if you let it. A lot of golf instruction is just that, which is too bad. For 99 percent of those who play, golf is purely a game, a form of entertainment. It seems to me that if playing golf is going to be fun, telling people how to play it well should be made as simple as possible. Truth is, even the pros, who play golf for a living, seek the same end. So that is my aim in this book and in every other form my teaching takes: to cut through complexity and find and explain the basic fundamentals of the golf swing.

A complicated theory of the golf swing, therefore, is just not in my bag. However, there is one aspect of method that might be called a theory if only because it represents the central theme behind all my ideas on the golf swing. I am referring to the address position. It is vitally important, and I will speak of it very often throughout this book (just as I do in my golf clinics and when working with the tour pros).

Trying to play golf with a poor address position is like owning a fine car that has a faulty ignition system. A couple of frayed or unhooked wires ruin all your potential for graceful and powerful movement. What is more, since a sound address system requires no special degree of strength or skill, or even good physical coordination, there is no reason

why every golfer cannot have one.

My premise is that the best golf swing is the one with the fewest angles. Angles start in the address position, which is based on an imaginary line running through the clubface to the target — the "target line" — and the relationship to that line of your shoulders, hips, knees, and feet. If other imaginary lines were drawn across those body parts, in a proper address position they would be exactly parallel to the target line. This is what is called being "square" to the target line.

You maintain the square position in the takeaway for the first 18 or so inches of the backswing. Then new angles form as the left knee cocks, the right arm bends, the wrists break, and the shoulders turn. These new angles are natural and productive ones — you could hardly swing the club at all without them. However, if you are in a faulty address position, you probably won't form these backswing angles as they should be formed, and you're likely to create others that have no good reason for being. Now you have put yourself in a situation where you must compensate, because for every deviation or bad angle there must be a counter-deviation or reciprocal bad

The perfect, "no angles" address position — imaginary lines through the shoulders, hips, knees, and feet parallel to the target line, which runs through the ball.

angle. More often than not, the club will contact the ball in such a way as to produce a poor flight pattern, and you will lose power because of insufficient clubhead speed at impact.

For example, if at address your right shoulder juts forward—perhaps *the* most common address fault among average golfers—you move the entire shoulder line so that it points to the left of parallel to the target line. You create an oblique angle, and almost invariably you will start the club back and up from the ball to the outside of your target line, instead of directly back along it.

If you then keep the club on the "outside" path in the downswing, you will either slice the ball to the right or pull it straight left of the target, depending on whether the clubface is open or square to the swing path. Let's assume, though, that you *know* the club should meet the ball while moving either directly down the target line or slightly from the inside. To achieve this with an "outside" takeaway, you must reroute the path of the club at some point late in the backswing, or at the start of the downswing. Even if you are successful, you are needlessly complicating the

The most common address fault: Right shoulder jutting forward moves shoulder line out of parallel to target line. Result is faulty outside to in swing.

SWING PLANE   TARGET LINE

action by creating one angle to compensate for another – the one formed by the jutting right shoulder at address. Both angles are destructive, as well as unnecessary.

I don't deny you may hit the occasional good shot with bad angles, but only the *occasional* one. I emphasize *occasional* despite the fact that as great a golfer as Ben Hogan distinctly rerouted his swing (although not because of a jutting right shoulder). The timing and control to make such mechanics work the way Hogan did takes an amount of play and practice the average golfer is simply not going to put out. On the other hand, Byron Nelson had the "straight-back, straight-through" golf swing I advocate (and tried to emulate, since Byron was my professional mentor), and he did not have to practice nearly as much as his great competitive record might suggest.

To do nothing about unnecessary angles is like having a bad lower back and doing no exercises to strengthen and stretch the muscles. Disaster can strike at any moment. Always remember that your address position is critical to the success or failure of every golf shot you'll ever hit.

I

ELEMENTS OF A SOUND ADDRESS POSITION

Aside from being square to the target line, the key elements of the address position are foot spread, knee flex, posture, and the balance that comes from these, plus an item that affects all the other elements more than most people realize – the distance you stand from the ball.

Byron Nelson always said, "You can't stand too close to the ball." Actually, you *can*, as Byron admitted, but he made his sweeping comment because he saw 99 percent of golfers standing too far from the ball and he wanted to get these people closer to it. The only golfer I've ever seen who even *looks* as though he is standing too close to the ball is Don January, and he is doing pretty well that way, and has been for a long time now.

Standing too far from the ball causes a number of things detrimental to good shot-making. First, your weight usually moves out toward the toes, which creates poor balance. Second, you'll tend to stiffen your knees, which destroys good leg action. Third, your posture will be poor – you will almost always slump forward with the shoulders, rather than flex at the knees. Like the jutting right shoulder, this reduces your chances of swinging the club on the best path.

How do you know when you are standing too far from the ball? If your feet flounder around after impact, you had bad balance at address. If you hit balls solidly but they don't fly the distance they should, you lost your knee flex. If you slice or pull a lot of shots, check your right-shoulder position.

There are other signs of standing too far from the ball at address. You are too far from it if both your arms are rigid, or the butt end of the club is more than 6 or 7 inches from your body. You are too far from the ball if you cannot wiggle your toes while at address because too much of your weight is on them.

AND YET. . .

The fascinating, and confounding, thing about all this is that most of the poor positions described above *feel good*. The farther out you stretch your arms and the more you stiffen your knees at address, the stronger and more powerful you're likely to feel. You also feel powerful when the right shoulder juts out, because it elongates the right arm—all the consequent stretching and tightening make you feel you can hit the ball hard and far. (Indeed, the urge to "kill it" frequently results in these physical manifestations.) Finally, a slumped back and shoulders feel more comfortable than a straight back and squared shoulders if only because the human spine has not

yet evolved to where it can easily support an upright body.

Getting up closer to the ball pretty much forces a more erect posture with a straighter back, some flex in the knees, and more relaxed arms, which for many golfers will create a sense of being cramped and weak. I believe it is fo. :his reason—probably more psychological than physical—that so many golfers fail to realize they are too far from the ball at address. Instead of going to the source, their setup at the ball, they erroneously blame their slices, pull-hooks, and other bad shots on secondary causes.

WHAT'S RIGHT AT ADDRESS?

All the negatives I've outlined above suggest the positive address positions. You should concentrate your weight back toward the heels of the feet. Keep your back straight as your body bends slightly forward *at the waist*. Flex your knees and position your knees, hips, and shoulders parallel to the target line. Your distance from the ball, measured by the space between your body and the top of the club shaft, should never be more than 6 or 7 inches.

This is what I call Plan A—the basic address position. Let me develop it in more detail.

Foot Spread

The tendency is to spread the feet too wide, once again because this gives a false sense of strength and stability. You can be plenty stable enough with the tried-and-true measurement — the insides of the heels no farther apart than the width of your shoulders. If you depart from this norm, I recommend only going narrower, because an excessively wide stance severely restricts proper use of the legs in the swing.

Ball Placement

Assuming the correct foot spread (shoulder-width), if you play the ball to the right of the center of the spread you will probably strike it with a too sharply descending blow. Teed-up balls will then be "skied" — hit too high — and those played off the ground will be hit "fat" — behind the ball.

If you play the ball left of center you are on safer ground. But too far left can be even worse than too far right. Play the ball off the left instep or beyond — which is not uncommon among average golfers — and you will probably hit it too much on the upswing, producing a very low flight and a lack of force.

Also, when you set the ball too far to the left, your right shoulder almost invariably juts forward, opening the entire shoulder line. This in turn causes the club to cut across the ball from outside to inside the target line, producing a pull or a slice. In fact, this is the most common cause of the slice.

Where *should* you play the ball? Traditional golf instruction says that with the short irons you should set the ball opposite the middle of your feet. Then, as the clubs get longer, gradually move it toward the left heel, where you position it for the driver, the longest club in the bag. I don't agree with this dictum. If you change the ball position for various clubs, you alter the point at the bottom of the swing arc where contact is made. In golf, you want a swing that's easy to repeat, so *for all normal shots, play the ball from the same position with all clubs.*

Each individual must find his own exact best ball position, but in general it will be just left of center between the feet. For me, it is just inside the left heel.

When you've found your ideal position in practice, the problem still remains of finding it during a round, when you cannot use training devices (such as laying down two clubs parallel to the target line, one across the toes, the other just outside the ball, and a third at right angles to the first two indicating ball position). Unlike when you are hitting balls on a practice range, just about every shot on the golf course is at a different angle from the target, and off terrain that rarely is level. This is a problem for golfers at every level of ability—which is why tour pros constantly check their ball position—and there is no simple or one-time solution. Proper ball positioning is a matter of muscle memory derived from constant play and practice, from working on this element of the set-up on every shot you play. If you get into the habit of properly positioning the ball, you will sense when it's wrong. When that happens, step back from the ball and start all over again. Not enough golfers do that, and they miss many shots as a result.

Hands Ahead?

Most golf instruction over the years has advised that the hands be set slightly ahead of the ball at address, especially with the irons. This is fine for the golfer who, as he swings, turns his body as if he were standing in a barrel. However, he must be careful not to open the clubface when moving his hands forward, a common move that greatly increases his chances of hitting weak shots high and to the right of the target.

I set my hands even with the ball with all clubs, because I don't swing in a barrel. In the downswing, I make a lateral slide with my body (before turning the left hip to the left), and my hand position is correct for this kind of action. I'll discuss the lateral slide later, and say here only that if you start with the hands ahead of the ball and *then* slide laterally, your hands will be too far ahead of the ball at impact.

GETTING INTO THE ADDRESS POSITION

In a way, I've put the cart before the horse by first describing separate parts of the final address position. However, if you start toward the ball without knowing your destination, the end of the journey is likely to be unhappy.

One of the most important elements of every golfer's game is how he approaches the ball. The process of getting into the address position creates a psychological/physical mood vital to the success of each shot.

Too many golfers come to the ball directly from the side, stepping up to it at a 90-degree angle to the target line. They must then twist the head and look over the shoulder to sight the target line and align the club to it. This type of sighting disorients them, and is the main reason why so many of them jiggle and twist so much once they are at the ball.

To take the correct address position, start from behind the ball facing the target (1),
then move to beside the ball following a crescent-shaped path (2 and 3).

Despite all this movement, these golfers often fail to set up square to the target line.

Another problem created by moving into the address position at a 90-degree angle is the tendency it produces to "reach" for the ball — to stand too far from it. Reaching promotes the three main faults at address: weight on the toes, knees locked, shoulders slumped with back rounded.

The *only* 100 percent effective way to get into the address position is the way the top players do it. Begin from behind the ball, directly facing the target. This gives you the proper perspective on where you want to go

—your eyes, the ball, and the target are all on the same line. Then move to beside the ball along a shallow arc to the target line. As you can see in the illustration, the shape of the path you take is a crescent.

The first "solid" position is taken with the right foot, which you place at a slightly oblique angle to the target line and slightly behind the ball. Next, put the club behind the ball with its face square to the target. Now, set the left foot in its final position at the same slightly oblique angle as the right foot, and with the ball in the proper position (a few inches inside the left heel).

Adjust the right foot by bringing it back no more than an inch or two so that both feet are parallel to the target line; do not take a big step backward with the right foot or you will get into a *closed* position, aligning your body to the right of the target. Finally, set the right foot at right angles to the target line (I recommend this position as a guard against swaying, which I'll discuss more fully later).

You are now in the prime address position. Check your alignment by laying a club down in front of your toes, then step behind the ball to face the target. The club should be exactly parallel to the target line.

Now let me give you what will almost certainly be a new image of your movement to the ball. You should feel like someone sneaking up for a peek around a corner, with your head tilted slightly to the right and the right side of your body bowed inward. The feeling you want is that of being "under" the ball. Personally, coming to the ball I sometimes feel a little like Groucho Marx making that funny, low-slung, knees-bent walk of his.

Bottom-Line Golf

After placing your right foot in its initial position, you set the clubhead behind the ball with its lower or leading edge perpendicular to the target line. Note that only *then* do you finally position your feet and body.

The opposite is to set the feet and body in their final positions, *then* try to align the clubface to the target. A lot of golfers do this, and it's the main reason why they're so inaccurate. By first setting the leading edge of the clubface in place, you establish a guide from which your body takes its positions. Just as the leading edge of the club is square to the target line, so too will be your feet, knees, hips, and shoulders. In effect, you are positioning your body relative to the bottom line of the clubface.

I have just presented many pieces of business that in total make up the address position. You can't possibly think of them all in the few moments it takes to make a single golf shot, and you should never try to. In this book, I'll cover the full range of my ideas on all aspects of the golf swing, but in trying my suggestions, do so only a couple at a time. When you are satisfied with those, go on to others. Practice each enough, and with a little patience you will eventually do them all automatically.

ADDRESS TIPS

• The natural tendency is to swing the club to where you are looking, not to where your body is aligned. For example, even though you align your body to the right of the target, you look at the target itself as you finalize your address. Your eyes tell you where you *want* to hit the ball, and your body then obeys their command. So, in this case, you will throw the right shoulder outward in the downswing — known as "coming over the top" — in an effort to get the clubhead moving along the target line through impact. More often than not, though, coming over the top results in swinging the clubhead from out to in across the target line through impact. Then you either slice the ball to the right or pull it to the left, depending on whether the clubface is open or closed to the swing path at impact. Good alignment means you must coordinate your *body alignment* with your *visual sighting*. Line up with where you're looking.

• When soling the club at address, let it just barely touch the top of the grass. This gives you more clubhead feel, reduces tension in the arms and hands, and allows a freer takeaway. Never, never "lean" on a golf club.

• When settling in at address, keep your feet moving slowly, as though you were marching in place, or wiggle your toes. These actions will help you keep from getting too rigid. Also, if you can wiggle your toes your weight must be correctly placed — back toward your heels.

• Totally *visualize* your address position before taking it.

• If your left knee is bowed outward, you are in a weak position. Cant the knee inward to get a firm arm-and-shoulder takeaway.

• Feel your upper arms snugly up against your torso when walking into the address position.

• By sticking your rear end out, you give yourself a better chance of getting your weight back toward your heels.

• When you're playing well, check your distance from the ball, your foot spread, and your ball position. Actually *measure* them, so you have three definite points of reference when your game goes off.

• Getting closer than usual to the ball and then backing off is better than the reverse procedure for finding your correct distance to stand from the ball.

• If you over-reach at address, your right shoulder *has* to jut forward. A jutting right shoulder is the biggest cause of poor swings for beginning golfers, and it's also the main cause of slicing and pull-hooking among golfers who've played a while but poorly.

II

GETTING A GRIP ON THINGS

Beginners in golf should not be given lessons on swing mechanics—or certainly not complicated lessons. This is especially important for young people, because their bodies are going to change and so will their coordination. However, right at the outset everyone should do his darnedest to acquire a sound grip that can be used for the rest of his golfing life. If you can make yourself walk around the house (and elsewhere) taking and holding that correct grip until it becomes perfectly natural, it will be very hard for you to change it as you play more. By the same token, if you start out with a poor grip, you are likely to be stuck with it forever, which will severely limit your playing potential.

Among experienced golfers, it is much easier to correct a poor swing than a poor grip. When I was younger I had a grip with the right hand a bit too much under the shaft, in the "strong" position. It worked fine for a long time, because I was playing a lot and practicing even more, and was cocky enough to think I could make anything work. Then I met Byron Nelson, and he had me put the right hand more on top of the shaft, in the "weaker" position. I said that wouldn't be hard to do. He disagreed. He said I would be conscious of my hand, that the shots I would hit with the new grip would not be my customary ones, and that I would want to let my right hand return to the old position. He was right. It took me two years to get that hand permanently where Byron wanted it. But the change was for the best, because it reduced my chances of hooking shots, and, when under pressure, of blocking out—that is, not releasing the right hand fully and thus pushing the ball to the right.

This story illustrates not only that it is hard to change an ingrained grip, but that about the only way to make a poor grip work is by playing golf constantly, as I did as an amateur. The average golfer is not going to give the game that much time, so if he hopes to play well he'd better start with a sound grip and stick to it.

With a good grip, you have a solid foundation on which to build the rest of your game, and you will be able to play good-quality golf all your life. In my experience, very few golfers have been successful with poor grips.

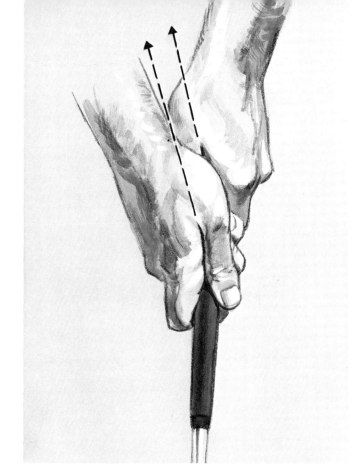

If the V's formed by the thumb and forefinger of each hand point to the right shoulder, you'll have the right amount of flexibility in the hands, plus the necessary control over clubface alignment at impact.

Vs FOR VICTORY

What is the basis of a good grip?

I subscribe to the time-honored rule of having the Vs formed when you close the thumb and forefinger of each hand point toward the right shoulder. It has proved out over many years that no matter what the conformation of a golfer's hands—long-fingered or short-fingered, thick or slender, strong or weak—the Vs pointing to the right shoulder provide just the right amount of flexibility in the hands, plus the necessary control over clubface alignment at impact.

If you become a strong-hitting, low-handicap player, you may decide to alter that basic formula, probably by "weakening" the left hand a little. Until then, stay basic. (I'll explain the terms "weak" and "strong," as related to the grip, a little further on.)

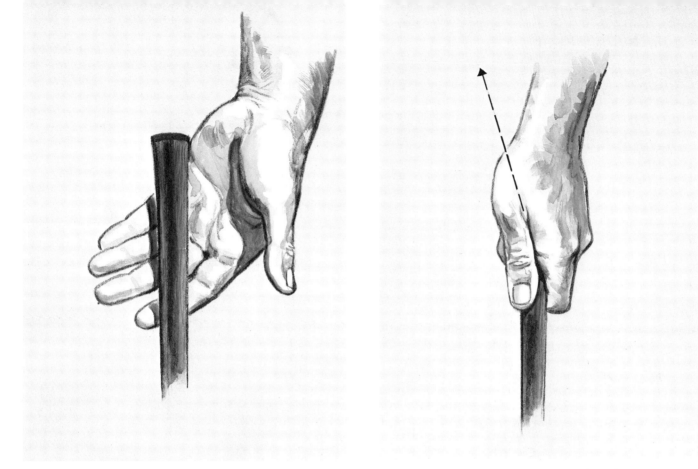

It is easier to point the V of the left hand correctly if you hold the club more in the fingers than the palm; you'll also have more clubhead feel.

In the Fingers of the Left Hand

It is easier to correctly point the V of the left hand if you hold the club *more in the fingers than the palm*; you will also have more club-head feel. Specifically, the club runs from the juncture of the palm and the last two fingers, across the lowest section of the middle finger and the middle section of the index finger. Other parts of the hand obviously will be on the handle, but you do the *real holding* at the points I've just described.

Your left thumb should ride just to the right of the center of the grip.

Right Easily Wronged

The right hand is the toughest to get on the club correctly, partly because of the overlapping or interlocking of its little finger with the left hand (which I'll discuss shortly), but also because the right hand is generally the dominant one and thus by instinct wants to position itself the way it feels strongest.

The right hand feels strongest when it is more or less under the handle, the way I had it before I met Byron Nelson. The feeling carries over from baseball, which most of us in the United States play before we take up golf. The ultimate "strong" grip would have the palm of the right hand facing the sky. Not many golfers go that far, but quite a few head in that direction. This kind of position feels strong because the club is held deep down toward the base of the fingers, almost in the palm, giving a great sense of security. It also produces strong shots, in that the right hand can more easily roll over at impact and send the ball on a right-to-left, hooking flight with a lot of run once it hits the ground. Overall, however, accuracy with a grip of this style is always questionable, because the rolling over of the right hand is extremely difficult to control consistently. Too often, the hand rolls too much and the ball hooks in like degree, either flying or rolling into trouble on the left side of the course.

With a strong right-hand grip, the V points outside the right shoulder. The ideal position has the palm pretty much facing the target, with the V aiming directly at the right shoulder. Now the club will lie much more in the fingers, giving you better feel and far greater clubhead control.

The right thumb should lie diagonally across the handle, with only the inside of the thumb in contact with the club.

INTERLOCK OR OVERLAP?

In a good swing, the hands work in unison, as though they were a single unit. To achieve that they must be more than just close together — they must be actually connected. You connect them with the little finger of the right hand, which either lies in the crevice formed by the index and middle finger of the left hand (called *overlapping*) or is entwined with the left index finger (called *interlocking*).

Players with particularly small hands tend to interlock, and among them a few will use the so-called ten-finger grip — pretty much the baseball grip except that the left thumb lies on the top of the handle, rather than around it. Art Wall, Bob Rosburg, Tim Norris, and Beth Daniel are among tour golfers who use the ten-finger grip.

As far as I'm concerned, though, the "best" style of grip is the one that works the best *for you*. Personally I prefer overlapping, because it puts one more finger on the shaft — the left index finger — and thus gives me more flexi-

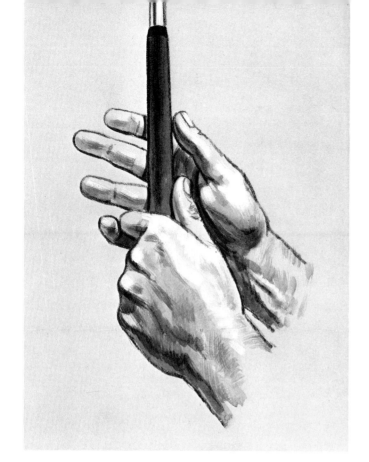 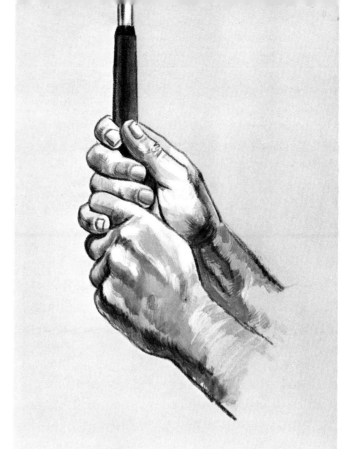

The ideal position of the right hand has the palm pretty much facing the target, with the V aimed at the right shoulder.

bility and feel. For me, interlocking seems to cut down a little on flexibility, but there's no question it does get the hands really close together. In fact, at times when my grip doesn't feel right for some reason, I will interlock to get that closeness, and then slip the little finger of the right hand into the overlap position. Such golfers as Jack Nicklaus and Tom Kite use the interlocking grip, so it can't be too bad.

The main point is that your hands must be closely and securely connected. Whichever style of grip seems to do that best for you is the one you should use.

A GOOD GRIP IS A SLICING GRIP...
IF YOU ALLOW IT TO BE

One of the many peculiar contradictions in golf technique is that a good right-hand grip position can cause slicing. There are two reasons for this. First, assuming the golfer is being persuaded not to place his right hand too far under the shaft, which most of us start out doing, he is likely to exaggerate and set the right hand *too much* on top. Now, when the hand uncocks at impact, the palm turns upward, the clubface turns in the same direction into an open position, and slice spin is imparted to the ball.

The second reason is that when you move the right hand more on top of the handle, very often you also automatically thrust the right shoulder forward. The shoulders are then open in relation to the target line, and this practically guarantees that you will swing the club back outside the target line. You then have to reroute the club at some point in the swing for it to be moving through impact along the target line, or from slightly inside it. This is difficult to do consistently, certainly for the average golfer. More often than not, the club remains outside the target line on the downswing and cuts across the ball, causing a slice or a pull depending on face alignment.

Almost all golfers would rather hook — even badly — than slice, because a hook has so much more power than the puny "banana ball." Thus, most golfers tend to reject advice on where to set the right-hand grip, preferring instead to keep it too far under the handle. Ideally, you should set the right hand so that its palm faces directly toward the target. Avoid positions in which the right palm faces predominantly toward the sky, or the ground.

Trigger It

If you took a pistol in the right hand, put your finger on the trigger, then transferred the hand just as it was to a golf club, you would have the *perfect* right-hand grip. You can hold a pistol correctly only one way, and so it should be with a golf club.

THE LEFT HAND: WHY WEAK IS "WEAK," EXCEPT FOR THE STRONG

I think most average golfers get confused when they hear about "weak" and "strong" left-hand grips, especially when they're also told that strong-hitting players often use the "weak" position.

The premise behind the term is that, accuracy aside, a drawn or hooked shot is stronger than a slice or fade. Not only does the right-to-left shot roll farther, but it *feels* stronger because the hands have rolled over at impact. This is not the case with the slice or fade.

Starting from the ideal grip position — with the V pointing toward the right shoulder — if you turn the left hand more to the right, or

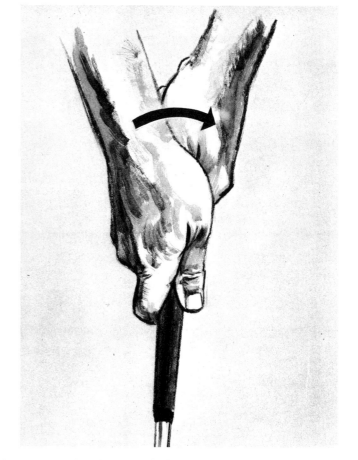

Starting from the ideal grip, with the V's pointing at the right shoulder, if you turn both hands more to the right (left hand illustration), this is termed a "strong" grip. If only one hand is turned to the right, then it is termed a "strong" position of the left or right hand. If you turn both hands more to the left (right hand illustration), this is termed a "weak" grip. If only one hand is turned to the left, it is termed a "weak" position of the left or right hand.

clockwise, on the handle, it is more suscep-tible to turning counterclockwise through impact – this "rolling over" is what produces a hooked shot. Thus, this is called a "strong" position.

The reverse positioning, with the left hand more to the left on the handle, makes the hands less likely to roll over through impact. Thus, because you can't hook as readily this way, the left hand is said to be in a "weak" position.

Low-handicap golfers often use – indeed, *need* – a "weak" left-hand grip, because, through playing a lot more than the average golfer, they have developed more "golf strength" in their hands, plus a generally more powerful overall swing that generates considerable club-head speed at impact. These two factors promote too much rolling over of the hands at impact, so to resist this they "weaken" the left-hand grip. They don't lose power because of their overall stronger swing.

It follows, then, that the average golfer normally should not use the "weak" left-hand grip position. If he does so, he will push or slice most of his shots to the right of this target. Also, even when he hits them on line, he will not generate maximum power – the shots will, indeed, be "weak."

The Knuckle Test

A good way of gauging the strength or weakness of the left-hand grip is to count how many knuckles of the hand you can see when you look down at your hands at address. If you can see only one knuckle, you are "weak." If you can see three, you are "strong"; if four, very strong. *I recommend the average golfer see two knuckles of the left hand at address.*

ON GRIP PRESSURE

Even the best hand placement can be ineffective if hand pressure on the handle is too great. An overly tight hold is more common by far than an overly loose one, and is due for the most part to anxiety. When we worry about the consequences of our shots, we tend to tense our muscles. When we have to hold something to perform, that tension almost invariably centers on the object we must hold. Thus, golfers who badly want to make a good shot – or avoid a poor one – tend to squeeze the club handle too hard. Their hands and arm muscles then become so taut that supple, smooth movement is impossible. Usually, the takeaway is a quick and jerky action that destroys any possibility of a smooth swing.

Another cause of holding the club too tightly is simply infrequent play. The once-a-week golfer usually doesn't develop much golf strength in his hands, and because he feels insecure when he does play, he tends to take a deathgrip on his clubs.

The solution to both these causes of excessive grip pressure is to play more often, or at least to get in some practice – range hitting or simply swinging a club between rounds. You will strengthen your hands for the game, and because more practice is bound to improve your shotmaking ability and give it more consistency, you will not be as anxious about your performance.

How to Know?

It is often difficult to know when you're holding the club too tightly, perhaps because the psychological tensions of golf are so great. But there are some clues. If you are hitting your shots solidly but aren't getting your best distance, you're holding too tight. If you find your hands become very sore, and/or your forearms ache after playing a few holes and certainly after an entire round, you're squeezing the handle too hard. You will also tire sooner than normally, because tension is exhausting.

Finding the Right Pressure

Everyone has his own level of strength, so finding the correct grip pressure is in large part an individual thing. One aid that I like is to squeeze and unsqueeze the hands a few times when at address, the idea being that you will subconsciously settle on the correct pressure when it is time to swing the club.

Another way I have come up with is to hold my hands together palm to palm with the fingers and the arms fully outstretched. Then the pressure of my hands is just right. However, if I cross my hands over so they are back to back — again with the fingers and arms outstretched — I feel too much pressure for good golf. Transfer the first feeling to the golf club.

The Final Test

The best single way I've found for getting the correct grip pressure, and one you can use in actual play, is to concentrate on just one particular pressure point, namely, the right palm pressing firmly against the left hand.

I've found that you can hold the club firmly with the fingers of each hand, but that the palms can still come away from the club during the swing. This never happens when you press the right palm against the left thumb.

GRIP TIPS

• I can correct most things in a golf swing, but it is very difficult to teach someone to fade the ball if he has a hooking grip (right hand under the shaft).

• Most of the left thumb should be on the shaft, so it can get tucked into the right palm and not slip off to the right or left under swing pressure. If you imagine a clockface on the butt end of the club, with 12 at the top center of the grip, I advise putting the left thumb just barely to the right of twelve.

• The length at which you place the thumb on the shaft is also important. If you want a longer swing, extend the thumb down the handle; for a shorter swing, shorten the thumb. Remember, however, that these are general rules, and that your natural flexibility may alter the formula. For instance, Sam Snead uses a short left thumb but, because of his double-jointedness and super-supple body, can still make a pretty long swing — even in his seventies.

• You may find it better to use a "weak" left-hand grip for short pitch and chip shots, and for putting, although you may not use that position for full shots. In fact, I recommend this practice. For these short shots you don't need power. You also don't want much, if any, release of the left hand. The weakening prevents such "wristiness," enabling you to hit through the ball squarely with the back of the left hand facing the target.

III

THE TOTAL SWING

I am going to talk first about the overall action of the swing before dealing with the two main parts—backswing and downswing—and other details. I do this because every golfer should have a mental image of his whole swing so that he can relate separate parts to a total picture. It also is essential to know the whole swing you're trying to make when you are working on the all-important element of tempo.

U IS IT

The shape of a fine golf swing is that of an *Elongated U*.

You form the Elongated U by keeping the club low during the takeaway and extending it as far back *on a straight line* from the ball as your physique allows. You do not, of course, extend the club to where your whole body is leaning away from the target.

The downswing is a return of the club along the backswing path, with the club moving down and through the ball. In this regard, think of the clubhead as a jet trail, the condensed vapor following directly behind a high-flying aircraft.

In reality, the swing will not form a perfect Elongated U from beginning to end. When the shoulders turn during the backswing, the club will move with them to the inside of the target

The shape of a perfect golf swing: An Elongated U.

line. And in the follow-through, the club will again swing to the inside of the target line. *But always swing with the perfect Elongated U in mind.*

That is the basic swing pattern — and mental image — for the mechanically inclined. For people with a more poetic turn of mind, I have another image. *Swing the club as though you were painting a big, solid fence,* using a large brush with both hands and with no fear of dripping paint. The brush and the motion of the arms and body have a rhythmic horizontal flow, what I call the Paintbrush Action.

Here I am talking not only about the shape of the swing, but of its "music." It is a complete composition, never a medley of different tunes. By this I mean that you must never break up the swing flow with "extra" acceleration of the club when it reaches the impact zone — that is, *with a hitting at the ball.* The word "hitting" is just about unavoidable in discussing the golf swing, but I wish it could be eliminated altogether, because all too often it is translated to mean "slugging." Instead of trusting the natural acceleration of a *swinging* clubhead to produce power — and maintain clubhead control — too many golfers feel they must add a *hitting* action. This almost invariably results in a rushed, inaccurate stroke. They don't strike the ball solidly, and its flight is erratic.

If this is what you tend to do, simply *consider the ball as an object that gets in the way of the swinging club.* You will immediately play much better golf. An illustration of this is the times you've missed a lot of shots during a round and then, when you get to the eighteenth hole simply wanting to get off the course before you hurt yourself, you played your best shot of the day. You did so because you weren't *hitting at* the ball, but *swinging through it.*

ON SWAYING

When you think about the Elongated U / Paintbrush Action, or just attempt it the first few times, you may feel you are committing one of golf's cardinal sins — that is, swaying, or moving your body too much from side to side.

Technically, you are swaying when, on the backswing, the right side of the body moves past your right foot, and on the downswing when your left side moves past your left foot. Another indication of a sway is when the right leg bows outward on the backswing, and the left leg bows outward during the downswing. Golfers tend to sway as a result of thinking that more body movement will create power. Generally, it has the opposite effect, because a

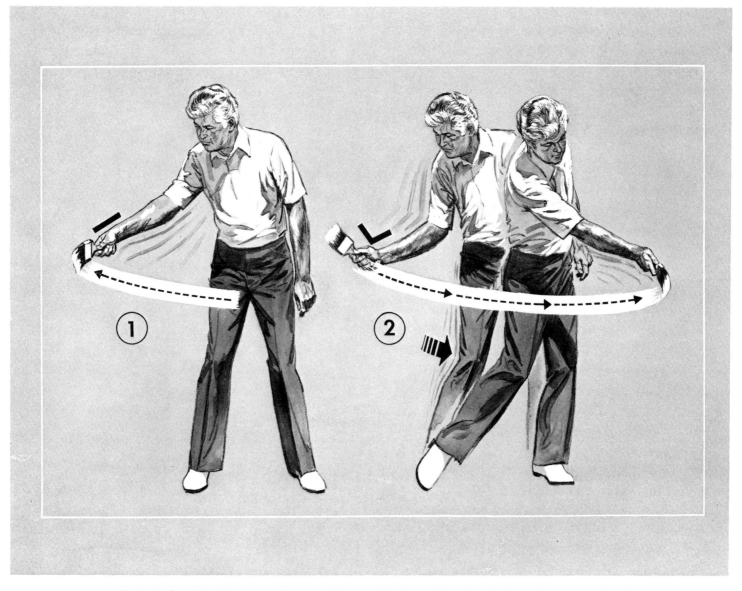

The "paintbrush" action creates the overall flow and rhythm of the swing. It also helps create a late-hit action, the hands leading the clubhead to impact.

swayer is swinging off an unstable, shaky foundation that, more often than not, produces mishit, inaccurate shots.

I will admit that the Elongated U / Paintbrush Action I advocate makes golfers susceptible to swaying. However, I believe that the overall value of my total-swing pattern overrides this potential problem. The Elongated U / Paintbrush Action is the most uncomplicated swing you can make, because it is a "straight-back and straight-through" action that requires no rerouting of the club.

There are two keys to prevent swaying. First, think of starting the backswing with only the right hand and upper arms and shoulders, with no movement in the hips (more on this later). Second, use your head properly. Here's an image—a feeling—I use to make my head work correctly in the golf swing. I imagine I'm wearing a catcher's mask and my face is pushing into it as the pitcher hurls the ball at me. The pitch is a fastball, and I have no intention of taking my eyes off it. With this thought I find my head stays as still as need be, as I swing my arms and body beneath it.

Another device I use to promote a steady head—and thereby eliminate the risk of swaying—is what I call "Chin-to-Chin." The thought here is to close the gaps between the right and left shoulders and the chin on the backswing and follow-through. On the backswing, I

To keep your eyes on the ball and your head steady, imagine you're wearing a baseball mask.

work on my left shoulder touching my chin, and at impact and beyond my right shoulder touching my chin. Chin-to-Chin not only helps keep your head in position, but also ensures

that you swing the club straight back from and straight through the ball.

TOTAL-SWING TIPS

• I like to tell my students that the practice swing is the taking of a photo, and that you develop the photo when you actually strike the ball.

• Ideally, if you were hitting a ball with your back against an imaginary wall, your back would not leave that wall; there would be no gap created between the two.

"Chin-to-Chin": A swing key to keep the head steady and eliminate a sway.

IV

THE BACKSWING

IT *IS* A RIGHT-HANDED GAME

The shape of the full backswing is half of the Elongated U. The most critical part of the backswing in creating that shape is the first 18 or so inches of the takeaway, when your clubhead *must* go straight back along the target line, and stay low – skimming just barely above the grass. You should execute this low, straight takeaway with a dominant right hand, which essentially *drags* the club back from the ball.

Emphasizing the right hand as I do here goes against the teaching of most other golf instructors, who say you must keep the right hand as passive as possible in the swing. They argue that because most right-handed golfers are right-handed persons, this hand is generally stronger than the left hand and so is apt to uncock too soon, robbing you of power, or roll over too much, especially in the downswing, causing badly hooked or pulled shots. Therefore, you must keep the right hand "quiet" in all phases of the swing. These teachers like to say golf is a left-handed game, meaning this hand should control the entire action.

I don't accept this idea. Because a right-handed golfer is almost invariably a right-handed person, I believe he can control this hand best and therefore should make maximum use of its strength and dexterity.

The takeaway: Drag the club away with the right hand as the shoulders and arms retain the "triangle" shape set up at address.

STARTING OUT

The dragging action of the right hand assures you that the clubhead will go back straight and low for the first 18 or so inches, and that the shaft and your left hand and arm will remain an unbroken unit in the takeaway. Your shoulders and arms move at the same time, but retain their address "shape," with the right shoulder a bit lower than the left (because your right hand is lower on the grip than the left hand). As the club goes back, do *not* allow your left shoulder to dip downward or the right shoulder to rise upward.

Your club is now on the right track, and the only body parts that have moved so far are your hands, arms, and shoulders. Lack of body movement from the hips down may make the action to this point seem rigid, but it won't *as long as you keep the knees flexed.*

As the club gets farther back from the ball, you must lift and extend it upward. The right hand, again, does the lifting. When the hands get to about waist-high, the right hand cocks the wrists in such a way that the right palm is facing straight ahead at a 90-degree angle to the target line. Your right elbow should point straight down to the ground.

When the hands get to about waist-high, lift and extend the club upward with the right hand.

If you're physically able, I recommend keeping the left heel down in the backswing. To get needed flexibility, cock your left knee to the right.

THE TURNING POINT

To achieve a complete extension of the club in the backswing—to get it back far enough to develop sufficient power—you must now set the rest of the body in motion. This begins simultaneously with the cocking of the wrists to raise the club.

Your right hip and shoulder turn as if on a swivel, but you must still have some "give" in the lower body to make a totally free-flowing motion. That "give" comes through a release of the left knee, which crimps or "moves" to the right until it gets about even with the golf ball.

The Left Heel—Up or Down?

You might increase the "give" provided by the kicking in of the left knee if you allowed the heel of the left foot to rise off the ground. Many golfers do this, including Jack Nicklaus, Tom Watson, and Ray Floyd. However, I seldom recommend it.

If you let the heel rise, you must lower it in the downswing. This up-and-down move adds another element to the always tricky problem of timing, especially when you're playing the longest clubs in the bag, which is when the heel would rise the most. Excessive heel lift could be one reason why Nicklaus, Watson, and Floyd constantly work on their driving.

Byron Nelson and Ben Hogan, on the other hand, were extremely accurate drivers and had no perceptible left-heel rise during the backswing.

Also, it is possible, when the heel rises, to get up on the toes of the left foot. This leads to a jutting forward of the left knee and a dipping down of the left shoulder – both of which produce poor angles.

I prefer to have the left knee move laterally during the backswing, with the left heel remaining on the ground. On the longest swings, the entire left side of the left foot may rise slightly as the ankle rocks, but that would be all. I believe this type of left-foot action will give you sufficient flexibility to make a full turn on the backswing, yet retain the proper stability in your lower body.

AND THE RIGHT FOOT?

In the matter of stability – having a good, solid foundation off which to swing the club – your right foot also plays a vital role. First of all, in the backswing there is going to be – indeed, there *must be* – a considerable shift of your weight to the right side; at the top of the backswing the ratio should be around 60 to 40 in favor of the right side. However, you must not "overshift" the weight so much that it goes to the outer edge of the right foot. If your right foot is tilting up on its outer edge, then you have overshifted and almost certainly swayed "off the ball." You then will have a difficult time shifting your weight correctly to the left side in the downswing. Only outstanding – and young – athletes can recover from a backswing overshift.

By starting the backswing as I have suggested, using only the right hand, arms, and shoulders for the first 18 or so inches, you reduce the chances of overshifting to the right. The turn of the shoulders and hips will be firm, and you will transfer your weight to the middle of the right foot.

An additional way to prevent an overshift to the right side is, as I mentioned earlier, by setting the right foot "square" at address – in other words, at a 90-degree angle to the target line. In this position, the right foot acts as a block against overshifting. At the same time, the square right foot keeps the right leg firm as it takes the shifted weight and the leg becomes a kind of springboard for beginning the downswing.

A word of warning on the right foot. You may be advised – or decide for yourself – that to prevent a sway you should concentrate pressure on the *inside* of your right foot while at address. Worse, you may put more weight on the left foot than the right at address and so stand tilted to the left. I see a lot of this among average golfers, and wish I didn't. Both positions are not only unnatural, they often lead to the reverse pivot; that is, during the backswing most of the weight remains on the left side, then on the downswing it shifts to the right side. This, very definitely, is *not* the way to play good golf.

You have taken the club low and straight away from the ball, raised it while turning your right shoulder and hips, and bent your left knee inward toward the right knee while keeping your left heel on the ground. About 60 percent of your weight has shifted to the middle of your right foot. Your right leg is firm, but retains its flex, as does the "kicked-in" left knee. Your head is serving as a fulcrum under which your body turns, and your chin is pointing at the ball. You have just about completed your backswing. All that remains to be discussed are, first, whether the plane of the backswing should be flat, upright, or somewhere in between; second, how far back you should take the club; and third, whether you should keep the left arm straight.

FLAT, UPRIGHT, OR WHAT?

A flat backswing is usually defined as one where the shaft of the club, at the top, lies outside the right shoulder. An upright backswing puts the shaft inside the right shoulder.

I believe golfers often put too much emphasis on this aspect of the swing. Your backswing plane should be a "happening," the natural result of your particular physique and muscle flexibility. It is very likely that if you're tall and thin and have long arms, you will have an upright backswing. Conversely, if you're short, heavyset through the chest, and/or have short arms, you'll probably have a flat backswing. Your backswing plane should take care of itself, and it will, provided you make a complete turn of your shoulders and hips and do not tamper with the plane that is natural for you. Only if you try to force the plane into some preconceived position—upright, to hit the ball higher, for example—when it does not suit your physique will you create improper angles.

LENGTH OF BACKSWING

The longest backswing a person of average proportions should ever make is one where the shaft of the club is parallel to the ground. In general, though, you should only swing back this far with the driver, the longest club in the bag. As the clubs shorten, your length of backswing should also gradually shorten

The length of backswing: Longest with the driver, shortest with the wedge.

until, for full shots with the 9-iron and wedge, the shaft at the top of the backswing is just past vertical to the ground.

The different lengths of backswing will tend to happen without a conscious effort on your part because the length of the club you're using will dictate how far back you swing it—assuming, of course, you do not try to "slug" every shot.

On Overswinging

However, if you're a person with especially small physical proportions, and particularly if you're a woman, you often will need to extend the length of your backswing with all clubs to generate more power. You may very well have to bring the shaft past horizontal, at least with the driver.

The danger in making so long a backswing is letting go of the club with the left hand, usually as the club swings past horizontal. If this occurs, you instinctively grab at the club with the loosened hand—regrip it, or "play the piccolo," as it's called. In doing so, you stand a very good chance of altering the angle of the clubface before it reaches the ball. Piccolo players are never consistently good strikers of

the ball, because the clubface is often not square at impact.

If you need to swing the club farther back than normal, allow *a little* more rise of the left heel than I advised earlier, *and keep your left hand firmly fixed on the club.*

THE LEFT-ARM QUESTION

The word people use most often to describe the condition of the left arm is where most of the trouble lies. Usually it is spoken of as a "straight" left arm, which the average golfer often translates to mean "stiff," or "rigid." *There is no place in the golf swing for anything that is stiff or rigid.*

It's true that if the left arm bends too much, you lose club extension and thus both power and accuracy—particularly if you don't straighten the arm at impact. However, if the arm is stiff or rigid, with the elbow locked, it restricts your body turn. You then must become too "wristy" a golfer in order to develop power, and give up consistent ball contact and flight control.

The left arm should make a good *stretch*, and remain firm throughout the swing. Forget the "straight left arm." Rather, think *firm left arm.*

The left arm in the backswing: Not locked, but firm.

TURNING ON: THE WAGGLE, ETC.

I have now described all the essential elements of the backswing. You might be able to put them into motion from an absolutely static position, but that is not advisable – and, in fact, this is one of the more subtle problems in the golf swing. The golfer has no reason to be moving before beginning a stroke, as does a tennis player, for example. However, starting the swing from motionlessness is not conducive to a smooth, rhythmic action. Generally, it produces an uneven, jerky start that prevents you from ever truly *swinging* the club.

Over the years, golfers have come up with a number of ways to create motion before launching into the swing. Some of them, in my opinion, are no better than the original problem. For instance, many golfers use the forward press—pushing the hands a little toward the target before starting the club back. I don't think this is wise, because you can change the position of the clubface, usually by opening it.

Among the game's top players, Lee Trevino moves his left foot laterally just before "turning on," whereas the trigger of Jimmy Demaret, Julius Boros, and Fuzzy Zoeller is to slide the clubhead forward so the ball is opposite the heel of the club. But these are tricky moves that can breed trouble for those who don't play a lot of golf.

There are golfers who cock or kick the right knee in to the left as a way to get into motion for the swing. Gary Player does this, and it's not a bad idea.

The most common way to get into motion is the waggle. The golfer sets the clubhead behind the ball, then lifts and drops it a few times. Alternatively, he lifts the clubhead and swings it over and past the ball before dropping the club back behind the ball. A moment after the last drop, the backswing starts. I don't like any of these, and for a very good reason.

My waggle is to swing the club back and forth behind the ball and *on the same level* with it, never letting the club rise above or go forward of the ball. Basically this is the same action a pool player makes, moving his cue stick back and forth behind the cueball and effectively simulating the stroke he will use to actually hit the ball. *That* is my "good reason." It seems to me pointless, and potentially destructive, to waggle the club in a way other than the way you want to swing it. You don't want to hit the top of the ball, or swing above it, so why waggle as though that is your intention? Why use a move you will not use in the swing proper?

The next-best solution to the problem of a static start is simply *not to stand at the ball too long*. The longer you stand at address without starting the swing, the more tense you'll get—psychologically and physically. Conversely, it's tough to "freeze" if, once you've made up your mind what kind of shot you want to play, you take your address position, waggle a few times, then "pull the trigger" immediately. Develop this routine and use it for every shot you play, both on the practice tee and on the golf course.

BACKSWING TIPS

• If you keep the right hand passive and allow the left hand to dominate the start of the backswing, you will probably cock the left hand inward and under. The club then tends to rise abruptly, with the back of the left hand and the clubface turning so they face the ground—not a good way to start a golf swing. Other effects of a passive right hand are that the left shoulder dips low while the right shoulder rises, and the right elbow juts backward instead of pointing straight down to the ground at the top of the backswing. In all, you create a number of very bad angles that require intricate compensations if you are to be in good position at impact. If you're a weekend golfer, you won't be able to make such compensations very often, if ever. So *drag* the club back low and straight with your *strong right hand,* and save yourself a lot of trouble.

• Many odd-looking backswings are the result of players' resisting what is natural to their physique. As I noted in my previous book, *The Venturi Analysis,* Ray Floyd and Miller Barber are two examples of this phenomenon. Both players should have flatter backswings than they do, because they are fairly thick-set through the chest and shoulders. But

The waggle: Swing the club back and forth behind the ball and on the same level with it—this simulates the start of the backswing.

both of them want to be more upright, Raymond to take more advantage of his height, and Miller because, as he says, "I just can't do it the right way."

Thus Floyd has developed a somewhat labored, angular-looking swing, and Barber cocks his left hand under when he starts the club back. Of course, both are superb players despite these unorthodox actions, in large part because they play and practice almost every day of their lives—as, indeed, they *need* to. The average golfer doesn't play or practice nearly as much, and so he must develop the *least* complicated swing possible. That is the purpose of this book: to give the average golfer a way to step onto the first tee on a Saturday morning, without having held a club all week, and still have a fair chance at a decent round.

• An effective practice routine for getting into the habit of taking the club straight back from the ball, and low, is to place a tee in the ground about a foot behind the ball on the correct path, with its top just barely above the ground. As you start back, try to graze the top of the tee with the bottom of the clubhead.

• When the right shoulder is rising too high in the backswing, it is often because you have too much weight on the left foot at address, which tilts the upper body to the left. This position restricts your shoulder and hip turn, and leads to a reverse pivot. One antidote, of course, is to distribute your weight evenly on both feet. Another I often suggest is to *pull the right shoulder back a little at address.*

V

THE DOWNSWING

THE PUMP-LAG AND SLIDE

The most common error that the average golfer makes as he brings the club down to impact is to misuse the lower body—or not to use it at all. He seems to think that because the hands and arms have brought the club up, they must also bring it down. That may seem logical, but in golf it doesn't work that way.

The "hands and arms" downswing also stems from a desire to *hit the ball*, rather than to swing the club *through* it. Once again, since the hands are holding the club, it seems logical that they should do the actual hitting in the downswing. Once again, it doesn't work that way.

Hitting is an aggressive act that excites us —we want to do it as soon as possible. Thus when we actively use the hands and arms in the downswing, the wrists almost always uncock too soon, usually as the hands are about shoulder-high. (Terms used to describe this early uncocking of the wrists include "casting" and "throwing from the top.") The results of early uncocking are a severe loss of power, and shots that slice to the right or are pulled to the left of the target.
Basically, what you want to achieve with the downswing is to keep the wrists in their cocked position until just before impact, when they finally do quickly release. However, you must

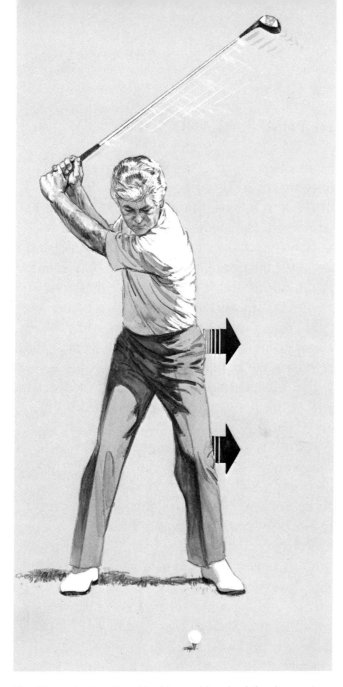

The "Pump-Lag" action: The hips and legs lead the downswing with a "pumping" action laterally to the left, with the hands and club "lagging" behind.

not force that release by overusing the right hand, but allow it to happen as a natural result of the momentum generated by the swinging of the club. Once the right hand has done its work in the backswing, both it and the left hand must become "silent partners" in the swing.

What should generate the downswing momentum of the club, while also eliminating conscious use of the hands, is lower-body action. Just *before* the club reaches the top of the backswing, the hips and legs begin a *pumping* movement to the left, with the hands and club *lagging* behind the lower body into the downswing. I call this the Pump-Lag Action.

The Pump Is a Lateral Slide

The *initial direction* of the pumping action of the lower body is *lateral*; it is a slide to the left on a line parallel to the target line. It is not a long slide, as I will show in a moment. The lower body will turn away from the target line eventually, but it does so only *after moving laterally*.

This brings me to a couple of phrases used by many golf teachers, and also by some analysts on golf telecasts, that I wish could never be heard again. They are "Get the left side out

A

B

A drill to learn the correct lateral slide: Set up in a doorway, with a six-inch gap between the left hip and the door jamb. With the first move of the downswing, the left hip will hit the jamb (A). If you "spin out," your left hip will turn before it reaches the jamb.

of the way" and "Clear the left hip." Far too many golfers think these phrases mean that they must turn the left side to the left *as soon as the downswing begins*. This is one of the most common faults in golf today, and a certain way to guarantee high scores.

If you get the left side "out of the way" *before* making a slight lateral slide, you tend to straighten the left knee and pull your body away from the ball. Golf teachers refer to this action as "spinning out." When you spin out, you thrust the right side of the body outward toward the ball, which in turn brings the club

across the ball from outside to inside the target line, causing a slice or pulled shot, depending on clubface alignment.

In fact, by getting the left side out of the way, you end up getting the right side *in* the way. Nothing good can come of this.

As I suggested earlier, I am not saying the left side should never turn away in the downswing, but that it should turn *only after the lateral slide*.

Here's how to teach yourself the feeling of the lateral slide.

Take your address position in a doorway,

The "Tug-of-War" drill gives you the feel of a solid downswing.

with the side of your left foot flush against the bottom of the jamb. There should be a space of about 6 inches between your left hip and the jamb. When you start the downswing, the left hip moves into the doorjamb. *That is the lateral slide – no more, no less.*

THE TUG-OF-WAR POSITION

When your left hip hits the doorjamb, your hands should have come down to about waist-high. If you were to freeze at this point you would be in the same position as someone pulling on a rope in a tug-of-war. It is an image I would like you to keep in mind, because it will help you achieve a strong and solid position at a critical point in the downswing. Your shoulders will be almost exactly as they were at address—that is, parallel to the target line, the right slightly lower than the left. Your right elbow will be close in to your right side. Your wrists will still be cocked as they were at the top of the backswing, with the heel of the left hand leading and aimed toward the target, and the shaft of the club vertical to the ground. A good practice drill is to assume the Tug-of-War Position while a friend holds the clubhead (see illustration).

THE FINAL KICK

To complete the downswing from the Tug-of-War Position, "kick" the right knee to the left — moving the right knee not outward toward the ball but directly toward the left leg and parallel to the targetline. With a proper full "kick," the right knee should be even with the ball when the clubhead strikes it, and the gap that previously existed between the legs should be reduced by half.

You will find that the "kick" of the right knee forces the left side to turn to the left as it should, away from the target line. The "kick"

To complete the downswing, kick the right knee in toward the left.

also generates the momentum in the clubhead necessary to uncock the wrists and cause the clubhead to strike the ball with the face square to the target.

DOWNSWING TIPS

If you've worked the right shoulder "under" correctly in the downswing, your head will feel as though it's lying on an imaginary pillow in the follow-through.

• To achieve the pump-lag lateral slide in the downswing, you must retain the flex of the knees from address onward. If you don't, you won't have the flexibility and mobility you need to use your lower body correctly.

• Because centrifugal force develops during the downswing, the body weight tends to move toward the toes. This tendency can produce two negative results. First, as your body leans forward, the club goes forward, too, and you shank the ball—with the irons you hit it with the neck of the club, and with the woods you catch the ball well back in the heel of the clubface. Second, knowing instinctively that with your weight forward at impact you might fall on your face (to exaggerate), you "save" yourself by reflexively pulling your body back at, or just before, impact. Then you pull the club back away from the ball and hit it with the outermost portion of the clubface—the toe—which is almost as bad a fault as the shank. These problems show why it is so im-

portant to have your weight back toward your heels at address.

• If you have made a good downswing, your right shoulder should have "worked under" so that in the follow-through you watch the flight of the ball with your head tilted to the right. I like to feel as though my head were lying on an imaginary pillow. If, instead, the right shoulder has moved forward toward the ball during the downswing—has come "over the top"—you will watch the flight of the ball with your head upright, and your eyes facing directly down the line of flight.

VI

REPRISE OF THE TOTAL SWING

I am going to present here a description of the basic, full golf swing as I conceive it, without many of the details included in the previous chapters. I think this will help you see the golf swing as *whole*. (The sequence photographs of my swing used here were taken in 1964, when I was at the height of my competitive career.)

At *address* you are "square," your feet,

The following sequence photographs beginning here and continuing through page 67 show any swing in progressive detail. They best illustrate any overall idea of a sound golf swing.

knees, hips, and shoulders parallel to your target line. Your weight is back toward your heels, your knees are comfortably flexed.

You *waggle* the club a few times, the clubhead moving back and forth *behind the ball* and at *ball height.*

You begin the *takeaway* by bringing the

club back low and straight away from the ball for about 18 inches. Your right hand "drags" the club back, and the arms and shoulders move in precisely the same direction. There is no movement of the body from the hips down.

The *backswing* continues with the right hand cocking the wrists at about waist-height

and lifting the club upward. At the same time, the right hip and shoulder turn as if on a swivel, and the left knee "kicks" in toward the right leg. The left heel remains on the ground as the middle of the right foot takes about 60 percent of your weight. Your left arm is not absolutely straight, nor is it very much bent. It is *firm*.

The *downswing* begins an instant before the club reaches the top of the backswing, with your hips and knees sliding about 6 inches laterally to the left.

About halfway through the downswing, your hands have remained cocked and 60 per-cent of your weight has transferred to the left foot.

To complete the downswing, you "kick" the right knee to the left.

At *impact* your hands have uncocked fully and are in the same position they were in at address. Your lower left side has turned away from the target line.

The clubhead is moving along the target line.

Your knees have remained comfortably flexed throughout the swing.

The shape of the whole swing is that of an Elongated U.

VII

TEMPO

The best golf swing in the world is not going to be very productive if its tempo is not right. "Not right" is a relative term, of course. All of us have an "inner clock," a certain pace at which we function most comfortably and effectively. Nonetheless, "not right" in golf almost always is a matter of swinging too quickly. I rarely hear of a golfer complaining that he is swinging too slowly, or a golf teacher telling a player to speed up his swing!

Tom Watson, for instance, is a person who walks and talks at an upbeat pace. His swing tempo is much the same, but it often ticks faster than his "clock." Tom has openly expressed concern about sometimes swinging the club too quickly. On the other hand, easygoing Sam Snead has never worried about swinging too slowly. All of this demonstrates that in golf, speed kills. If you're swinging too quickly, it's very difficult to complete the necessary turns and shifts of a full golf swing, or to stroke with finesse in the short game.

Many overly fast golf swings are the result of psychological tension, anxiety, and self-doubt. They can even come from indecision. For example, a golfer may not be sure he has enough club for the distance he must hit the ball, so he rushes the swing, thinking that by swinging faster he will get more distance.

Everyone has experienced tightening of muscles and numbing of nerve ends when worried about something, especially a physical performance. The fear is of failing — and, sometimes, even of succeeding. Golfers are particularly prone to these fears, and out of them come overly fast swings that invariably feature a jerky takeaway and a shortened backswing. Conclusion: Those who can most often complete the backswing with a nice full turn of the shoulders stand the best chance of maintaining proper swing tempo.

How can you overcome anxiety and tension? More play, and practice, can help. The weekend golfer is going to make more fast swings than the one who plays three or four times a week, because he is less sure of what he is doing. But more golf is not a certain remedy; even touring pros swing too fast on occasion.

If you're an average golfer who does not play or practice much, you must begin slowing down even before you get to the course. The game's greatest players have done this, in an effort to build up a reservoir of good tempo. Ben Hogan, who always fought a fast swing, made a point of driving to the course well under the speed limit. Walter Hagen took a half hour to shave, and reached for objects — salt shaker, a drink, a golf club — as though he had all day. Bobby Locke very consciously slowed his walk, his speech, his every action as he prepared for a round.

It is not always easy to know you are swinging too fast. If your "inner clock" has been ticking rapidly for a while, a fast golf swing is going to seem natural. A friend in your foursome can tell you if you're rushing the swing, and if he says so, *listen to him*. Also, if you are hitting a lot of shots "thin" — catching the ball near its "equator" with the bottom of the clubface and thereby hitting it very low — you are probably swinging too fast.

MECHANICAL SOLUTIONS

Are there any "mechanics" that can help you swing with a better tempo? No one I know has come up with a definitive one, but I have a few things to suggest that have helped me.

I've mentioned that a full turn of the shoulders in the backswing can help you slow your tempo. The probable reason is that a full shoulder turn is the result of an evenly paced takeaway, which in turn has an even earlier genesis. So I will go back another step or two in the swing.

I have always felt tempo is related to how you work your feet while getting into, and standing in, the address position. Somehow, you cannot move your feet slowly and swing the club too quickly. Indeed, a clue to an upcoming fast swing is that in taking your address, your feet are jumping and bouncing around as if you were standing on hot coals. If you ever catch yourself doing this, step away from the ball and start all over again – slowly. Walk to the ball with a nice "one-two-three" rhythm. Also, get your weight back toward your heels to give you the sense of balance and stability that will also promote relaxation.

The waggle can be another "early warning" of too fast a swing. If you're moving the club up and down or back and forth like a hot piston, you're almost sure to make too fast a swing.

Sam Snead's preparation for a golf shot sums up a lot of what I have suggested here, and he also suggests another. For his practice swings before getting into address, Sam never took a full backswing or follow-through. He made a half-swing, which simply cannot be done quickly. In this way he was injecting a good tempo into his system. He completed the job by not being in any rush to get into address or to set his feet in position. Finally, Sam's waggle was a long, deliberate one with a pause at the end (and with the club never going above or forward of the ball, either).

Here's one more suggestion, which is not mechanical but an indirect yet truly valuable way to develop good tempo. We are all imitators, often subconsciously. So, if you happen to be playing with a golfer who has a fast swing, *don't watch him*! If you do, you may very well end up swinging at his pace rather than your own. By the same token, if a playing partner has an easy, well-paced swing, watch his every move. You might even go out of your way to get into his foursome. That was the case with George Fazio, when he was a tour player back in the Nelson-Hogan-Snead era. George had a beautifully rhythmic swing, and the other pros – including Hogan – did whatever they could to play at least their practice round with George.

VIII

ON PRACTICING THE SWING

It very often happens that when golfers begin to play below their usual standard, the problem is not a fault that has developed in the swing itself, but a fault that has developed in the address position. Oddly enough, this often happens when they are playing their best.

The better you are hitting the ball, the stronger you feel both mentally and physically. The usual physical manifestation of this, if you normally play from a square setup, is that you begin to close your stance and reach for the ball, because these moves make you feel even stronger. Before you realize it, you are too closed at address, and reaching too far for the ball. Poor swing angles result, and then you start to make compensations in the swing to correct them.

So, the most important thing you can do in a practice session is to check your alignment at address. Do it often during the season, and do it whether you are playing well or not. Have your pro or a friend stand behind you looking down the target line to confirm that you are aligned as you should be. Often, the golfer – even the tour pro – is the last to know he's out of position.

Practice requires discipline just as much as playing, and you should always practice with definite objectives in mind. Just beating balls out can do you more harm than good. Once you're satisfied your address position is sound, think about what you want to do with your swing before every shot. Also, simulate golf-course conditions. Always have a definite target on the range and play "shots" to it – a hook, a fade, a low ball, a high shot, and so on.

It is time to quit practicing when your mind begins to wander, and you're no longer trying "shots" or thinking about your swing. It is better to practice for an hour with your mind tuned in than to beat balls mindlessly for three hours.

IX

THE
SHORT GAME

The short game involves any shot that does not require a full swing.

In a way, the short game is the most interesting part of golf because of the variety of shots possible, and it is certainly the most important in making good scores. A well-struck full golf shot gives much pleasure, and can satisfy the power urge we all have, but in the end it is the short game that really makes the score. Even the world's best ball-strikers will tell you that.

To me the short game embraces a wide range of shots from distances of around 75 yards to a couple of feet — pitches, chips, sand shots, putts. The various techniques for these often differ from the basic full swing I have outlined, but not entirely. There are some fundamentals that apply to both the long game and the short game, and are vital to the success of each. Before getting into the different short-game shots, therefore, I want to make sure you know these fundamentals. As you might imagine, they mostly have to do with the address position.

It may not seem important that you have a solid foundation for short shots, since the swing is so much less forceful than for full swings, but in fact balance and stability are even more crucial. The slightest movement of the body on a little chip shot or a 3-foot putt can cause a miss, whereas you might very well get away with it on a swing with a driver. So, for all short shots, *keep your weight well back toward your heels* at address.

Knee flex is another essential fundamental, for both the stability *and* flexibility you want, in particular for pitch shots. You can't drive your knees, as I will describe, if you have them locked at address.

Short shots — especially the little chips from just off the greens, and the putts — have a way of making us hunch over at address like a jeweler fixing a watch. In fact, poor posture for these shots is the main cause of hitting them "fat" — that is, behind the ball. *Good posture* — a straight back, a slight bend at the waist — is as essential to a good short game as it is to hitting long straight drives.

THE PITCH SHOT

For shots from 75 yards in, length and tempo of swing are both reduced. Unfortunately, it is impossible to teach anyone how to coordinate a visual sense of distance with the length and tempo of swing that will get the ball close to the pin. Each golfer must learn this from experience. However, I can teach you how to make consistently solid contact with the ball, so that you have a dependable base from which to judge how hard or soft to hit pitch shots.

Of all the short-game shots, the pitch from, say, 75 yards down to about 40 yards comes closest in technique to the full-swing shot. You play the ball a little inside the left heel, with the hands lined up even with the ball. You start the club back low and straight, with only the hands, arms, and shoulders moving, and moving as a unit.

However, your right hand must cock a little sooner — below waist-high — to lift the club, and the turn of the hips and shoulders, the length of the backswing, and the crimping of the left knee to the right will all be less than for a full shot. All these elements will be *in proportion* to the length of the shot you are playing. The longer the shot, the fuller the turn of the shoulders and hips, and so on.

The downswing begins with a slight shift to the left by the hips and legs — a miniature Pump-Lag Lateral Slide action — but with a slight difference. The lateral "kick" of the right knee begins a *little earlier*, because of the shorter backswing. When you time the "kick" properly, your knee will arrive exactly even with the ball at impact. My mental image for this is to imagine a pair of cymbals tied to the insides of my knees. Then, I aim to "clang" them at impact.

Your wrists must uncock *naturally* at impact, and you want the club moving straight out after the ball to complete the Elongated U.

The pitch shot swing is essentially the same as the full swing except that the right hand cocks a little sooner and the swing is shorter.

To time the right knee "kick" correctly on the pitch, I imagine a pair of cymbals on the insides of my knees, and aim to "clang" them at impact.

You also should be watching the flight of the ball from "under" your right arm, with your head tilted to the right "on the pillow."

Spinning It

The ultimate success of most pitch shots is measured by how quickly the ball stops after landing. In fact, of all the short-game shots, the pitch from 40 to 75 yards is the one with which you have the best chance of getting a ball to spin backward after the first or second bounce, because you are making a hard enough swing to impart plenty of backspin. From inside 40 yards, that sort of backspin is almost impossible to achieve even for the best players.

You need proper conditions to get good backspin, even from the optimum distance. For example, the finest golfers in the world will not be able to spin a pitch shot backward if they are playing from deep rough, or a lush fairway, or from wet grass of any length, or to a hard-surfaced green. To get such backspin, the ball must be sitting up on close-cropped grass with a firm base, and hit to a green that is relatively soft, or that at least has some "cushion" of grass. It also helps if the green tilts a little toward you, and you're playing into a breeze — no one is going to "spin it back" with a strong tailwind.

To take advantage of the ideal conditions, two elements in the basic swing are critical. First, your takeaway must be low, and second, your right knee must "kick" left.

The low backswing creates the Elongated U swing shape that produces a pitch with a fairly shallow trajectory, one that comes into the green at an angle about that of an airplane nearing touchdown. It may come as a surprise to you that I advise a shallow trajectory, because most golfers believe that the best trajectory for making the ball stop quickly and spin back is a high, looping arc. Such a flight will certainly make the ball stop reasonably well, but in order to achieve it, you must take the club back on a steep angle and then bring it down with a sharply descending stroke. This V-shaped swing is harder to achieve consistently well than the Elongated U that I recommend.

With the V-shaped swing, the tendency is to hit down too sharply, often behind the ball. Also, with the slightest overshift of weight to the left, you hit on top of the ball. Either way, the results will be poor.

The other temptation in going for a high-arc pitch shot is to try to help the ball into the air by "scooping" it. To scoop, the right shoulder usually dips very low in the downswing, and the clubhead is rising as it reaches impact. Poor angles are created, and the shot rarely works well. Usually, you "thin" or top the ball.

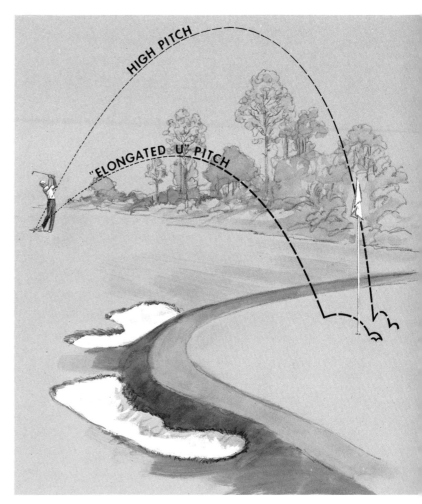

The "Elongated U" swing with a pitching club gives you a low trajectory and much more backspin than a "V-shaped" swing with its high, looping arc.

Since the ball does not have to come into the green from a great height in order to stop quickly, why change your basic swing shape? Stay with the Elongated U.

The right-knee "kick" is vital to ensure both the correct release of the hands and square contact with the ball. If you hold the right knee back, the right hand is forced to roll over the left at impact, closing the blade and imparting a hooking, running spin to the ball.

THE SAND-WEDGE PITCH: WATCH THE BOUNCE

It has become fairly common practice to use the sand wedge for standard pitch shots from about 25 yards and in, from grass. This is a good idea, because the club is a bit heavier than the pitching wedge and also has a little more loft. Therefore, you don't have to ease up on your swing or choke down on the grip as much as you would with a pitching wedge, and you will produce high, soft shots.

Some words of caution, though. For its primary purpose, playing out of sand, the sand wedge is made with "bounce," which can cause trouble when you use it from grass.

A club has "bounce" if the back edge of its sole is lower than the front (or leading) edge when the club is set down at address; the sole inclines from the leading edge to the back, a slope you can see by holding the sole level to your eye with the toe of the club pointing directly away from you or toward you (see

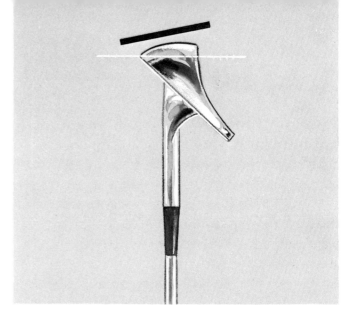

A club has "bounce" if the leading edge is lower than the back edge of the sole.

illustration). Another test for bounce is to sole the club on a hard floor. You know the club has bounce if the leading edge is not flush with the surface of the floor, as it would be with all other clubs.

A sand wedge is manufactured this way to keep the leading edge from digging too deeply. Instead, the lower back edge of the sole hits the sand first, limiting the depth of cut while enabling the club to "bounce" through the sand beneath the ball.

Now, when you're playing a sand wedge from grass and especially tight turf with no cushion, that "low" back edge of the sole tends to bounce off the grass, and when it does so the raised leading edge strikes the middle of the ball. The shot then will have a low, line-drive trajectory rather than the soft, floating shot you want—and will surely go too far. This is even more probable if you open the blade at address, because this adds even more bounce to the club.

So, if you use the sand wedge for pitch shots, *do not open* the clubface. Keep the blade square, or even "hood" (de-loft) it just a little to take the bounce off the club altogether. You still will get plenty of height on the shot, because of the large amount of loft built into the club.

THE PITCH-AND-RUN

We don't use this shot as much in the United States as they do in Great Britain, for example, because for the most part our courses have softer ground and more greens protected in front by bunkers or water hazards. Nevertheless, the pitch-and-run is a shot worth having, especially if the courses you play have very large greens or greens with wide, fairly flat openings. I also recommend the pitch-and-run for the high-handicapper; it's a good percentage shot for him because it doesn't require quite as much ball-striking precision as the pure pitch.

To play the pitch-and-run, you land the ball well short of the pin, allowing it to run along the ground most of the way to the hole. You

hit the ball lower in the air, of course, and therefore must use a club that will produce both a lower trajectory *and* run. Generally, you should select a 5-, 6-, or 7-iron for the shot. However, you can take an 8-iron if you're within 6 or 7 yards of the green and the pin is in the front portion of the putting surface.

At address, play the ball just to the right of the center of your feet, with your hands a little forward of the clubhead. This position promotes the low trajectory you need. The swing is made primarily with the hands, arms, and shoulders. There is little body movement or weight shift, except on the longer shots from, say, 40 to 50 yards. In the backswing, the right hand should create only a slight cocking of the wrists. The backswing itself will be rather short; your hands should not go back much farther than waist-high, and that only for the longer shots.

As I mentioned, the pitch-and-run does not require the precision of a pitch shot—you usually can get away with a slight mishit. You also don't have to fly the ball close to the pin and put backspin on it, as you do with a regular pitch shot. However, it still takes experience to judge how far the ball will run after it lands. You must consider how hard or soft the ground is, and the effect of any undulations. If the ground is hard and/or you're playing downhill, land farther back from the green

The pitch-and-run: A shot played with a lower-lofted club to land the ball short of the green and then have it run onto the putting surface.

than normal; if the ground is soft and/or you're playing uphill, land closer to the green. You must also "read" the terrain. If the ground slopes from left to right, aim to land the ball farther to the left than if the ground were level; if the slope is right-to-left, aim farther to the right.

THE LOB

If you are anywhere from 2 to around 15 yards from the green and you must carry the ball over heavy rough or a bunker, and the hole is very close to your side of the green, the shot you need to hit is a lob, this being a soft pitch that lands on the green like a butterfly with sore feet.

The club you use for the lob depends on the lie you have – how your ball is sitting on the grass. Because of its weight, a sand wedge is best from a good lie – the ball resting high on cushiony turf – or from long, heavy grass. However, if the lie is tight – the ball sitting low or on hard ground – you are better off using a pitching wedge. A key ingredient of the lob is opening the clubface at address, and if you do that with a sand wedge you'll raise its leading edge to the point where you could, from a tight lie, catch the ball in its equator and "skull" it low and long. There is no such risk with the pitching wedge.

At address, play the ball just left of the center of your feet and open your stance by drawing your left foot back from the target line. Also, spread your feet a little wider apart than normal. This wider stance will give you a low, wide swing arc, with the club moving into impact on a shallower angle of attack than normal. Rather than hitting down on the ball with a sharply descending blow, you want to "slip" the clubface under it, as though you were sliding the club under a door.

To lob the ball, make the swing almost entirely with the arms and shoulders. For the shorter shots, swing the club back and through totally stiff-wristed – as though your wrists were in plaster casts. For the longer shots, allow a slight cocking of the wrists so as to get the distance you need.

On all lobs, however, *never* allow your wrists to roll over through impact. Hold them firm right into the follow-through. In this way, you keep the blade open and get the "soft" shot you want.

THE CHIP SHOT

You play the chip shot from just off the edge of the green and up to about 5 yards back from it.

In a way, the chip shot is a miniature version of the pitch-and-run. The essential difference is that on a chip, you can — and should — land the ball *on* the green rather than short of it. In this way, the ball gets the truest possible bounce before it begins to roll to the hole. You want all chip shots to avoid the longer grass between the ball and the green, but at the same time start the ball rolling as quickly as possible.

That is why you should use a less-lofted club, such as a 5-, 6-, or 7-iron, for most chips where you're over 30 feet from the hole and have only a few feet of fringe to carry. Don't make the mistake of using lofted clubs such as the 9-iron or one of the wedges for such shots — with these clubs it is too difficult to control the amount of roll you will get.

I don't rule out using the more lofted clubs for certain chip shots, though. If you are playing downhill, or have only 10 or 15 feet of green between the fringe and the hole, then you *should* use a pitching wedge so that you can carry the ball onto the green and have only a little roll afterward.

Whatever club you use, the technique is the same. Grip down on the shaft so you get maximum feel and control of the clubhead, and reduce your overall grip pressure a bit for better touch. Set the blade squarely at the target.

Make the swing for the chip primarily with the arms. Feel as though you're "raking" the ball toward the hole. The action is very similar to the stiff-wristed swing I spoke of for the lob shot.

THE GREENSIDE SAND SHOT

The average golfer tends to be a poor bunker player for two reasons. First, he mistakenly thinks he must hit down into the sand behind the ball with a steeply descending stroke, ends up digging too deeply, and thus nullifies the "bounce" built into his sand wedge. Second, there's too much body movement in his swing, and too much shifting of the weight from side to side.

The well-played sand shot requires the club to strike the sand behind the ball at a very precise point. Excessive body movement and weight shift will severely worsen the chances of hitting that mark.

My method for playing the normal sand shot solves both problems. The key element is the wide spread of the feet at address — wider than for any other shot. In fact, I have the inner edges of my feet outside my shoulders on these shots, yet I still feel comfortable enough to function properly.

The extra-wide stance prevents any significant body movement or weight shift during

CHOKE DOWN

The chip shot: From just short of the green, use a less-lofted club to carry the ball over the fringe; allow the ball to run to the hole.

the swing. The stance also widens the arc of the total swing, so that you swing the club through the ball on a shallower angle than on normal shots. This is an "Ultra-Elongated U" swing, if you like, and thereby you eliminate the problem of digging too deeply into the sand.

Now, let's look at the entire procedure for playing the greenside sand shot.

Along with the extra-wide stance, dig your feet down into the sand for stability, and to get a sense of the sand's texture and depth. (Remember, it's against the rules to touch the sand with your club at address, or in your takeaway.) To compensate for the lowering of your feet, grip down on your sand wedge.

Play the ball more forward in your stance than normal, up off your left heel to help you hit into the sand behind the ball.

Open your stance by aligning your feet, hips, knees, and shoulders on a line left of your target. If the target line were 12 o'clock, your body would be aligned at about 10 o'clock. However, do *not* lay the clubface too open, as many golf instructors advise. Keep the bottom edge of the clubface almost square to the target — at 12 o'clock.

Swing the club primarily with the hands, arms, and shoulders. Again, contrary to much golf instruction on sand play, do not try consciously to take the club back outside your tar-get line. With the setup I'm recommending, it is unnecessary, and is yet another cause of digging too deeply. Simply swing the club back along the line established by your body alignment. Here's why.

Because you've aimed your body to the left of the target, you will naturally swing the club up outside the target line and then down across the ball from out to in. However, you've set the clubface square to the target, but open in relation to your body. Therefore, the ball will fly straight to the target, but you will get all the loft and cut spin you need to keep the ball from rolling too much after landing.

Aim to hit the sand about 1½ to 2 inches behind the ball. Because of the wide stance and swing arc, the club will slip under the ball and take a relatively shallow divot.

A good mental image to use is of the ball sitting on a tee stuck in the sand, and on the downswing of *splitting the tee in half*. In fact, you can *actually* do this as a way of practicing the shot.

Buried in the Sand

When the ball is buried in the sand — or "plugged," as it's often called — it's extremely difficult to control distance precisely or apply much backspin. So don't try to get "cute" with

EXTRA WIDE STANCE

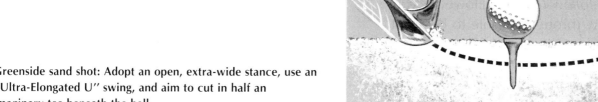

Greenside sand shot: Adopt an open, extra-wide stance, use an "Ultra-Elongated U" swing, and aim to cut in half an imaginary tee beneath the ball.

these shots or you'll leave the ball in the sand.

Your *sole* goals must be to get the ball *out* of the sand and *somewhere* on the green. They are not difficult to accomplish, provided you make the necessary changes in technique.

As on the normal greenside sand shot, spread your feet extra wide and dig them well down in the sand. On buried lies, however, take a slightly less open stance and play the ball just to the right of center of your stance, *so that you position your hands ahead of the ball at address.* Also, concentrate most of your weight on your left foot. These changes set you up to make the steeper swing you need. You want to bring the club into the sand on a sharply descending angle.

You should also use a square clubface on buried lies. With the clubface square, and your hands ahead of the ball, you nullify the "bounce" on your sand wedge, so that the club will cut deeply down into and through the sand.

Again, swing the club mostly with the hands, arms, and shoulders, and aim to hit the back edge of the crater around the ball. You must *think follow-through.* However, your actual follow-through is liable to be short because you are beating down rather severely into the sand.

These shots invariably run a long way after landing, so allow for that. And, I repeat, don't get cute.

THE FAIRWAY BUNKER SHOT

While on the subject of sand, let's discuss the fairway bunker shot.

Here again, your primary concern is to get out of the sand, so it is important that you use a club with enough loft so that the ball clears the front lip of the bunker. That may not be enough club to get you to the green, but being a little short is far better than staying in the sand.

You definitely want to hit the ball first on this shot, so play it far enough back in your stance to ensure clean contact, and choke down on the club in proportion to the depth you set your feet in the sand. To avoid hitting "fat," you must stay as steady as possible over the ball during the swing — try to keep your weight shift from side to side to a minimum.

Remember that a fuller swing demands more range of movement, so don't use the extra-wide stance here. Instead, stay flat-footed throughout the swing. Concentrate body pressure downward into your feet, and, to get the power you need, use more upper-body coiling action going back. As long as you keep your

On a fairway bunker shot, play the ball back enough in your stance to insure clean contact. Try to draw the ball most times by closing your stance—pulling the right foot back a little from square—and closing the clubface slightly. The closed clubface helps insure catching the ball first.

knees flexed, you will find you have enough lower-body flexibility.

In my case, I can stand flat-footed and hit the ball almost as far as when I swing normally. However, most golfers find they need at least one club more than usual when swinging flat-footed.

Note for Advanced Golfers: I'll be covering fading and drawing the ball later, but here I would like to point out that I very rarely try to fade a ball from a fairway bunker. I might try to do so if the pin is tucked on the right of the green behind a bunker, but my "standard" shot from a fairway bunker is a slight draw. That's because when you draw the ball you hit it more solidly and can squeeze a little extra distance out of whatever club you're using.

PUTTING

I am well aware that there are almost as many styles of putting strokes as there are golfers, and that putting is the most individualistic technique in the game. But that is precisely the reason why so many people have problems with their putting. Because it appears that "anything goes" on the green, golfers feel free to adopt putting techniques that differ radically from those they use in the rest of their game — to ignore fundamentals, in fact. This approach can and does make the shortest, least complicated, and least exertive stroke in golf become the most frustrating.

My views on the putting stroke are diametrically opposed to the "free and easy" school. I firmly believe you should think of the putting stroke as merely a miniature of the full golf swing, and therefore your fundamentals basically should be the same in both. (The few exceptions I will deal with later.)

Back to Basics

When addressing the ball to putt, again set your weight back toward your heels, with your knees comfortably flexed, and bend at the waist while keeping your back straight.

Stand with your shoulders, knees, and feet square to the line of the starting direction of the putt, and play the ball a few inches inside your left heel. Your foot spread can change, just as long as you feel comfortable.

Now, you will obviously stand closer to the ball in putting than for any other shot in golf, because you are using the shortest club in your bag. However, guard against the tendency to stand so close that your line of vision, when looking straight down, is "outside" or beyond the ball and target line. This is not a good position, because it gives you a distorted view of the ball and the line to the target, as well as throwing you off balance; you end up looking back at the ball as though, to exaggerate, it were between your legs. A better proposition is to position your head so your eyes are looking down on the top center of the ball. Keeping your weight back toward your heels aids this, but you should also check your eye line frequently.

One good way is first to address the ball, then either suspend the putter with the butt against the bridge of your nose, or literally drop a ball from the bridge of the nose. If the ball drops onto the ball you are going to putt, you are in exactly the correct position.

The ideal putting stroke is straight back from the ball and then straight through – simply the Elongated U without the upward curves at the ends. The putter head should move as if in a "trough," the blade remaining square to the target line at all times and it should be kept level to the ground on short putts. On longer putts – over 20 feet – the blade will rise somewhat on the backswing, but only *as a natural consequence* of the distance you must swing the clubhead in order to generate momentum.

Your hands, arms, and shoulders, working as a single unit, should move the putter, with

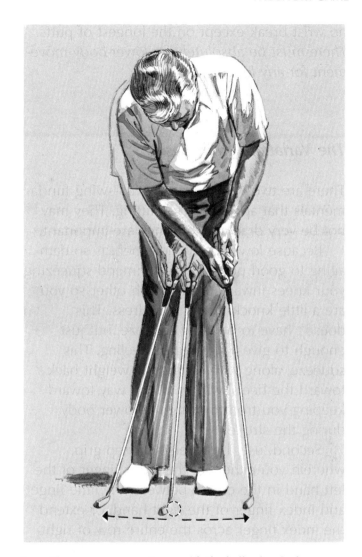

In putting, use a square stance with the ball a few inches inside your left heel. Swing the putter with your hands, arms, and shoulders working as a unit. There should be no lower-body action.

no wrist break except on the longest of putts. *There must be absolutely no lower-body movement for any length of putt.*

The Variations from Basic

There are two variations from full-swing fundamentals that apply only to putting. They may not be very dramatic, but they are important.

Because lower-body movement is so damaging to good putting, I recommend squeezing your knees inward toward each other so you are a little knock-kneed at address. This doesn't have to be a big squeeze, but just enough to give a "locked-in" feeling. This squeeze, along with setting the weight back toward the heels, will go a long way toward keeping you from moving the lower body during the stroke.

Second, use the reverse-overlap grip, wherein you either set the index finger of the left hand in the crease between the little finger and index finger of the right hand, or extend the index finger acros the entire row of right-hand fingers. This grip helps to keep the left wrist firm—it prevents the wrist from breaking down through impact, a prime cause of putts pulled to the left of the hole.

The reverse-overlap grip is not secure enough for hitting full shots, but that is not a problem with the less forceful stroke used in putting.

Finally, your grip pressure for putting should be a little lighter than for full-shot swings. This will increase your clubhead feel, giving you better touch.

Finesse Factors: Reading the Greens

Reading a green involves three basic factors. First, there is the slope of the ground between your ball and the hole—whether you are going to putt the ball uphill, downhill, sidehill, or over level ground. Second, there's the speed of the green—how fast or slow the surface is—which is the main factor in determining how hard you must hit the putt. Third, there's the grain of the grass, or the direction in which the grass grows.

There is little I or anyone else can teach you about how to play an uphill or downhill putt. Obviously, you hit the ball harder for the former than for the latter. If you consequently have difficulty hitting these putts the proper distance, then try using your imagination a little more. On downhill putts, putt for an imag-

AIM AT SPOT

For side-hill putts, pick a spot where the you think the ball will begin to turn toward the hole, then hit the ball directly at the spot.

inary hole short of the cup; on uphill putts, putt for a visualized hole beyond the cup. This mental trick helps a lot of people.

When the ground slopes to the right or left, a professional definitely can help. First of all, you should read the break of a putt one time only, by squatting low behind the ball, head erect, and looking directly down the line of putt. A lot of golfers like to take this "read" from the opposite direction as well – looking back at the ball from beyond the hole. I seldom recommend the "two-read" method because you will often end up seeing two different lines to the hole. When this happens you become confused, indecisive, and tentative.

If you can't see the break of a putt from behind the ball, take a close look at the hole itself from directly above it. Often you can see that one side of the hole is worn more than the other because of balls taking the break and hitting that side. Obviously, then, the putt will break to the worn side.

Now, many average golfers fail to realize that on putts with a sidehill break, the degree of break the ball will take depends on the speed at which it is rolling. The faster the ball is rolling, the less it will break, and this is especially important to understand when reading longer putts. You should be much more concerned about how much break there is within a 5-foot radius of the hole than at the start of your putt, because the ball will be moving faster when you hit it but will be moving very much slower when it gets within that 5-foot radius.

Once you've judged how much to allow for any sidehill slope, identify a spot on the green where you think the ball will begin to turn toward the hole. Then line up your body and putter blade at that spot, and hit the ball to it. Do this and you are, in effect, always playing a dead-straight putt. This keeps your thinking simple and direct, and enhances your chances of making a firm, decisive stroke.

One last word on break: If your first putt runs by the hole, don't indulge in "body English" or acts of disgust or anger to the point where you fail to observe the roll of the ball. Often, you can see the exact break of your next putt. Don't miss out on this vital information.

Judging the speed of greens is the most inexact of the three basic factors I am discussing. Nevertheless, there are "pro" techniques for getting a sense of the speed. For instance, when you walk onto the putting surface, feel how hard or soft it is through your feet. And if you're not the first to putt, watch the roll of the other players' putts all the way to the hole.

Reading the grain of a green is much easier than judging speed, because you can actually see grain. Look closely at the grass to find which way the blades are growing. The ball will always roll more easily in the direction the blades lie. Thus, if the blades are lying to the left in relation to the putt, the ball will break with the grain to the left. As a rule, if the ground slopes from right to left, the grain will run in the same direction – the tips of the grass will lie to the left, following the direction of water run-off. However, there are times when the grain goes against the slope, and in that case you must allow for less break.

If the grain is facing you, there will be resistance to rolling, and you must hit the ball a little harder than normal. If the putt is with the grain, the ball obviously will roll faster, and therefore you must stroke it a little easier than normal.

It's worth noting some other ways to detect the direction of grain. If the sun is out, and the grass appears shiny to you as you read the putt from behind the ball, then you're putting with the grain. If the grass appears dark, the putt will be against the grain. If there's a strong prevailing wind in your area, then very often the grain of the grass will run in the same direction as the wind. Grain also tends to run away from mountains or hills, and toward the ocean. Lastly, if all else fails, again *look at the hole*. The side of the hole that's worn from balls hitting it will show the direction of the grain. Also, you often can see the grass starting to grow over the side of the hole – usually in the afternoon and on toward evening. The direction of the grain will be from the "grassy" side toward the "worn" side.

Practice Putting

No one practices putting as much as he should, perhaps because it is boring compared to hitting shots with the irons and woods. I can understand this, since I never practiced putting nearly enough, even when I was playing the tour. In retrospect, I wish I had practiced more on the greens. It truly is where you make your score.

Assuming you are going to do as I say, not as I did, I have found a few practice-putting techniques that I believe are invaluable. These are aside from first reading greens and then stroking putts as though you were actually putting during a competitive round, which is rule number one for beneficial putting practice.

Find two spots on the putting green that are fairly close to each other – say a foot or less apart. Set your ball in the middle of them, then stroke it while making sure the center of the putter blade goes directly over the spots on both the backstroke and forward stroke. This is a fine way to get into the habit of making a straight-back, straight-through stroke.

Another way to practice the fundamentals of the stroke is literally to putt in the "trough" I referred to earlier. Get two 2-by-4s of wood about 4 feet long and set them down parallel to your target line and a little more than the length of your putter's head apart. Now putt in the "trough" until you can repeat the stroke without hitting either of the 2-by-4s. As your stroke improves, narrow the space between the 2-by-4s until it only just exceeds the length of the putter head.

Another idea is to practice putting occasionally with the leading edge of a pitching wedge, or with a training putter that has a head no bigger than the golf ball. In each case, you will be forced to concentrate on striking the ball solidly, and will get your mind off the hole and knocking the ball into it. I say this because one of the secrets of good putting is to forget the hole once you have decided on the line you want to take to it. Thinking of the hole really means thinking of the consequences of making or missing the putt, which spells anxiety. First, read a putt, then concentrate solely on making a solid stroke. This is the best way to avoid putting "nerves." After you determine the line, distance is the most important factor.

X
SHOTMAKING With Special Material for the Advanced Golfer

Shotmaking is the art of dealing with special situations on the course—situations that require you to do something "different" with the ball, such as hit it lower or higher than usual, or make it turn in the air to the left or right. To me this is the most interesting part of golf because of the infinite variety of "plays," not to mention the challenges that the execution of these shots presents.

Most of this chapter covers the basic shot-making repertoire—the hook and the slice, playing from downhill or uphill lies, and so on. I also include variations on some of these shots directed mainly, although not exclusively, to the low-handicap golfer. In these cases, the techniques I recommend call for a degree of ability to control the clubhead and to make subtle adaptations in the golf swing that comes from many years of serious, high-quality golf. This ability to finesse the swing is what distinguishes the advanced golfer from the tyro.

The shots and techniques for the advanced golfer are signified with a bold star, thus: ★

Please note that I am not saying that if you're an average golfer you can't have a look at this material. You may very well be approaching the stage in the development of your game when you can try some of these subtleties. If not, you can at least get an idea of what will be in store for you later.

Nor is this to say that if you're an advanced golfer you should ignore the material not specifically directed at you. At this game everyone — and I mean *everyone* — needs periodic reviews of things he already "knows." Also, I think there may well be a fresh idea or way of explaining something here that can add a little more understanding and finesse to your basic shotmaking.

THE HIGH-PERCENTAGE CURVES

The ability to curve a golf ball through the air with control doesn't merely satisfy an aesthetic sense. Very often, these can be the highest "percentage" shots — that is, the shots with least risk — you can make.

For example, let's say the pin is tucked behind a bunker in the back left corner of a green. If you hit the ball straight for the flag, you have only one safe side on which to miss the shot — the right. If you hit the ball even a little to the left, you'll miss the green and finish in the rough, another bunker, some kind of trouble. However, if you *start* the ball out to the right and then draw it to the *left* so that it's moving *in to the pin*, you now are working

with the *entire width* of the putting surface. If you get no draw at all, the worst that can happen is that your ball will end up on the right side of the green.

THE HOOK

A hook is a shot that curves in the air sharply from right to left. The advanced golfer may already know the basic technique for hitting this shot — at address, align the whole body to the right of the target, and roll the right hand over through impact — but I'm going to give him a refresher course anyway, and also add some vital pointers that are rarely taught, one of which is the correct way to get into the address position.

Getting into Address

Earlier in this book I mentioned that the way a golfer moves into his address position establishes a psychological and physical "mood" that's critical to the success of the shot. This is especially true when curving shots from right to left, and vice versa.

On all shots, you start from directly behind

LINE TO SECONDARY TARGET

ADDRESS

IMPACT

HOOK

To hook the ball, aim to the right of target, open the clubface and adopt a "strong" grip. Then roll the right hand over the left in the downswing to close the clubface.

the ball to get the best perspective of your target. But for the hook – and the draw – I want you to be a foot or so to the left of the ball as well as behind it. This may seem very subtle, but the fact is that starting from the left side of the ball greatly improves your perspective on the upcoming shot. Now you are not looking so much at the target itself – the center of the fairway or the pin – but at the secondary target to the right of it where you actually want the ball to head for at the beginning of its flight. Thus, your body tends to take the correct alignment for the shot – that is, set parallel to the line to your secondary target.

Probably the commonest error made by average golfers when attempting the hook is hitting whatever obstacle they're trying to work the ball around. Most often, this error comes from an incorrect alignment that begins with their approach to the ball. Instead of starting from a position to the left of the ball and behind it, as I've just suggested, they start from a point directly behind it, looking along a line toward the ultimate target. When they preview the shot from this position, it's almost impossible to visualize the proper starting line, and thus they end up aiming too close to the obstacle, with disastrous results.

The Address and the Swing

In gripping the club to hit a high hook, open the face slightly, then adopt a "stronger" grip with both hands. Turn the left hand to the right enough to see at least three knuckles. Move the right hand to the right also, or more under the handle of the club, so that the V formed by the index finger and thumb is pointing outside your right shoulder.

Now align your entire body – shoulders, hips, knees, and feet – parallel to the line to your secondary target. Set your hands a little forward, so they are ahead of the ball; this position helps you swing the club back on the same line as your body. Do *not* try to take the club back more to the inside than usual, a common mistake. You swing back normally and *make the hook in the downswing*.

With the club moving back to the ball along the line of your body, you roll the right hand over the left through impact to close the clubface; it feels as though the toe of the clubface is passing the heel. The closed clubface in relation to your swing path puts the hooking spin on the ball.

Why an open clubface at address? Simply because it triggers the proper downswing action, whether you're an advanced player or not. If you set up with a square clubface, your strong grip might trigger the rollover of the right hand, but then again it might not, because of what you're seeing in your mind's eye. However, when you *see* that slightly open clubface at address, you *know* you must have it closed at impact, and, knowing that, you *will* roll the right hand – every time. As a result, your intentional hook always comes off.

Why not simply close the clubface and take your normal grip? Many teachers claim that this is the "easy" way to hook a ball. I disagree. It *can* work – some of the time – *if* you can convince yourself to make a normal swing with a normal release. But too often, if you're an average golfer, a closed clubface will make you swing back outside the target line, and then up. From there the natural reaction is to swing down across the ball, again with a blocking action, which opens the clubface, leaving the ball out in right field. If you're an advanced golfer, you have a better chance of making this method work, but looking at a closed clubface puts a strain on your golfing instincts, which tell you to square the face at impact. If you do, you fall into the same error as the average player.

Believe me, I've tried all the methods there are. For my money, the only surefire way to hook is the stronger grip/open clubface combination.

★ THE DRAW

The draw shot also curves from right to left, but much less than a hook. That's why I like to call it a "soft hook." You use the draw not so much for going around trouble as for accuracy with safety.

For example, when the pin is on the left side of the green and there is water guarding the green from the left front corner down the entire left side of the putting surface, the safe way to approach is to play the ball well wide of the water and have it turn in toward the pin, If you can also keep the ball from rolling after it lands, so much the better.

The shot you need to hit here is a draw.

Start into the address position from behind and slightly to the left of the target. At address, align your body to the right of the target, but not as much as for a big hook.

Use your normal grip, and set your hands

either even with the ball or slightly ahead of it, whichever is your normal position. Also, open the clubface slightly, as you do for the hook.

The main difference between hitting a draw and a hook is that you keep the hands almost entirely out of the action. The right shoulder does the main job for the draw. On the backswing, turn the shoulder away a little more than you normally would. On the downswing, bring the shoulder "over the top" – that is, move it a little forward or toward the ball. Coming over the top will make you swing the clubhead down a line more directly at the target. That, plus an advanced golfer's instinct to square the clubface at impact, will produce the draw – a shot that will swing only gently from right to left.

If you want more draw, also rotate the right forearm counterclockwise at impact.

Why do you keep the hands "quiet" for the draw, but not for its big brother, the hook?

Remember, the hook is basically a trouble shot for which you need a sharply turning ball. You can get that kind of flight only by rolling the hands over at impact, a fast, aggressive action that produces a shot with similar characteristics. The draw, on the other hand, is an "accuracy" shot and takes more subtle mechanics. Thus, you draw the ball with the upper body, keying on the right shoulder. These bigger muscles will, by their nature, move slower than the hands.

For the draw, the downswing has a kind of slow-motion quality, which is reflected in the flight of the ball – a soft, floating trajectory that yields a minimum of roll after landing.

CLUB SELECTION FOR THE HOOK AND THE DRAW

For the hook, use the same club you would use for the distance if you had a straight-in shot. Because of the sharp turn the ball is going to make, it will not stay in the air as long as usual. However, the considerable roll of the ball after landing will compensate for that. A word of caution: If you think you can hook the ball and have it land on the green with a particular club, use one less club than that, land the ball short of the target, and let it run up to the pin (assuming, of course, there's a clear path in front).

For the draw, use one less club than the straight-in distance calls for. Because of the "over the top" action in the downswing, the draw is always a stronger shot than a straight ball.

THE SLICE

The slice does not turn as sharply in the air as the hook, but makes a high sweeping curve to the right. Even so, the genuine slice is still much more of an "escape-from-trouble" shot than its little brother, the fade.

For the slice, as for the hook, I have some ideas that are different from what is usually taught. They have to do with getting into the address position, gripping the club, and positioning the clubface at address.

To hit a slice – or a fade – move into address from behind and a foot or two *to the right* of the ball, to get the visual perspective that *says* to start the ball to the left of the target. At address, align your entire body – shoulders, hips, knees, and feet – well left of the obstacle you must work the ball around.

I recommend you use a *strong left-hand grip* to slice, contrary to most instruction. Turn the left hand to the right on the handle so you can see three knuckles when you look down from the address position.

Weaken the right-hand grip by turning this hand leftward on the handle so the V formed by the thumb and index finger points at the center of your chest.

Set your hands slightly ahead of the ball, and keep the *clubface square* (i.e., aiming along a line parallel to your body line). Do *not* open the clubface, as so many golfers are told to do, because if you do the ball will begin to slice too soon and you may not clear the obstacle.

You put slice spin on the ball with the backswing-downswing path, plus the action of the hands at impact. On the backswing, take the club to the outside – away from your body – then swing it down along the same path so that at impact your hands will be close to your body. With this swing path, you will cut across the ball from out to in, which imparts the required left-to-right spin.

The hands are very important to this cutting-across action. In the downswing, the *heel* of the left hand leads and should be past the ball at impact. The strong left-hand grip I recommend positions the hand to make this move right from address. You might think the left hand would roll over to the left when the ball is struck, but the "weak" right hand counters the "strong" left hand and prevents any rollover.

In effect, for the slice you don't use the hands, in that they do not uncock at impact. The feeling is more that of pulling a saw across the ball.

LINE TO SECONDARY TARGET

ADDRESS   IMPACT

SLICE

To slice the ball, set up well to the left of target with the clubface square. Adopt a "strong" left hand grip, but "weaken" the right hand grip. In the downswing, feel as though you're pulling a saw across the ball.

★ THE FADE

Hitting a fade takes more subtle mechanics than hitting a slice, plus those special golf-swing instincts I expect from the advanced player.

Approach the ball from behind and slightly *to the right*. Line up your shoulders, hips, knees, and feet to the left of the target, but not as much as for the slice.

Use your *standard left-hand grip*, even if it's a "weak" position. However, *set the right hand just a bit more on top* of the handle than you would normally – the V formed by the thumb and index finger pointing about to your right breast. Keep the *clubface square to slightly closed* at address, and your hands lined up even with the ball, or even a touch behind it.

On the backswing, *do not take the club to the outside*, or away from your body. Let the club follow the line of your body, which of course is aimed to the left of your target. Swing the club down on the same path, and you naturally will be cutting across the ball in relation to the actual target line.

It is in the downswing that the special finessing goes on that creates the fade.

Remember, at address the clubface is square to closed slightly, to prevent the ball from shooting to the right as soon as it is struck. So, during the downswing you work the clubface back to an open position with your hands, so that the heel of the club is slightly ahead of the toe as it passes through impact.

The "weak" right-hand grip aids in this opening action, as the hand will tend to return to its normal position with the V pointing at the right shoulder.

To prevent any possibility of the hands turning over, "kick" the right knee laterally to the left in the downswing. These mechanics, combined with your well-honed clubhead control and golfing instincts, will result in a shot that curves gently in the air from left to right.

CLUB SELECTION FOR SLICES AND FADES

These shots, by their nature, are not as strong as the hook and draw. The ball generally will not carry as far, and rolls much less after landing. Thus, for both the slice and fade, use at least one more club than the distance requires for a straight-in shot. You might use two more clubs for a slice that must make an especially wide curve from left to right. In any case, never try to power-hit a slice or fade, using your normal club for distance. You will surely swing too hard and risk turning your right hand over. Then you'll pull-hook the ball rather than slicing or fading it.

THE HIGH BALL

Usually, you use the high shot either to go over an obstacle or because you simply must hit a higher-than-usual approach, say to an elevated green. All you need do is make two simple adjustments to your basic address position.

The first adjustment is to grip the club slightly longer than usual: The heel of the left hand should just lap over the butt end of the grip. To understand how this adjustment makes the ball fly higher, you need a little background in clubmaking. If you were to lengthen a golf club physically — by inserting a plug in the butt end and then regripping the club — it would make the head feel heavier and increase the flexibility of the shaft. You should also realize that as a general rule, a club with a more flexible shaft will give the ball a higher trajectory, because of more whip, than a club

with a stiffer shaft. Thus, by "gripping longer" you in effect make the shaft slightly more flexible, and can obtain a higher shot than usual.

The second adjustment for a high shot is a wider stance. Take your standard address position, and, while keeping your hands even with the ball, widen your stance a few inches by *moving only your right foot laterally to the right*. Keep your left foot in place!

By widening the stance in this way, you start your swing with a little more weight on your right side, and, as a result, you will hit down on the ball less steeply than usual.

These two adjustments together produce a higher-flying ball without your having to make any real change in your basic swing. However, because of the wider-than-normal stance, you must concentrate on making a full shoulder turn going back.

I stress keeping the left foot in place when widening the stance because if you move the left foot to the right so the ball is lined up off the left heel or toe (as so many golfers do), the ball is going to be forward of its normal position when the clubhead reaches the bottom of its arc with your standard swing. To compensate for this, you must shift more weight than usual to the left side in the downswing if you are to hit the ball solidly. Even if you did this

To hit a high shot, grip the club slightly longer than usual and widen the stance by moving just your right foot to the right.

effectively – which is difficult, because it is a departure from the norm – you'd be making a move with the body that exactly counters the high ball you desire.

If you make no such correction in your swing, you'll either hit the ground behind the ball or hit the ball "thin" – strike it at or above its equator with a rising clubhead. Both types of contact result in poor shots and low shots.

My way is a lot simpler. Just move the right foot back, keeping the left foot in place, and swing as usual.

As for club selection, if you hit the high ball as I recommend, you will not need more club than normal for the distance. You will make solid contact with the ball, and get both the length the club is designed to produce and the higher trajectory.

THE LOW BALL

The low shot – also called the "knock-down" – minimizes the effect of a strong wind blowing into your face or across your line of flight. Into the wind, the "knock-down shot" won't climb

To hit a low shot, choke down on the club and widen your stance by moving just your left foot to the left.

too high and stay short of the target; in a crosswind, it will hold its line beautifully.

To play the low ball, you make just two adjustments at address: the basic principles discussed for the high ball, but in reverse. Choke down on the club a little, and position your hands slightly to the left of where you normally set them at address. Then widen your stance a few inches by *moving only your left foot* laterally to the left, while *keeping the right foot in place.*

By choking down on the club, you effectively stiffen the shaft a little, giving you a slightly lower trajectory. By placing a little more weight on the left side, you are set up to hit the ball with a slightly more descending blow than usual, again lowering the ball's trajectory.

I stress keeping the right foot in place while widening the left foot at address to get a low ball for the same reasons you should keep the left foot in place when setting up to hit a high ball. If, on the low ball, you move the right foot laterally to the left at address, which many golfers do, the ball will be too far back in your stance. In the downswing, the club will descend too sharply on the ball, driving it up into the air.

As to club selection for the low shot, always use one more club than you normally would for the distance. Why, for example, play an aggressive 8-iron shot that will reach the green only if you hit it absolutely perfectly when with a 7-iron you can make an easier, more controlled swing? Also, with the easy 7-iron you *know* you'll get the distance you need, *and* the lower trajectory. Tempo is very important when playing in the wind – the tendency is to rush the swing – so taking a little more club can help temper that impulse.

DOWNHILL, UPHILL, SIDEHILL

As I have said before, directly and indirectly, to me the address position or setup is at the heart of every golf swing we make. And so it is with shots played from uneven lies.

The main concern in playing these shots is to adjust your body to the terrain. This you do, primarily, by adjusting the address position.

Downhill Shots

On the downhill lie, follow the same procedure at address as for hitting the low ball. Take your standard position at the ball, then move the left foot a few inches laterally to the left – down the hill. Also, position your hands a little farther forward than normal – just ahead of the ball.

Now your body, and especially your shoulders, will have the same tilt as the ground from which you are playing. Your backswing will then naturally follow the slope. In other words, you can make your standard backswing and downswing *without* having to lift the club abruptly to clear the high ground behind the ball.

A lot of golfers pick up the club on downhill lies and very often hack down across the ball. They take the club up outside the target line, and slice these shots far right of the target.

As to club selection, a downhill lie will reduce the loft of the club you're using – a 3-iron's loft becomes like that of a 2-iron, and so on. Many golfers don't realize this fact and choose a club for the distance as though they were playing from level ground, then hit the ball too low. Another thing they don't recognize is that going downhill, 175 yards, say, usually *plays* at around 165 yards.

Therefore, for downhill lies use at least one club *less* than you would require if you were playing from a flat lie.

HANDS
AHEAD

From a downhill lie, widen your stance by moving just the left foot to the left. Use a more lofted club than usual.

Uphill Shots

For the uphill lie, reverse the procedure for the downhill lie. After taking your normal position at the ball, move the *right* foot a few inches laterally to the right, or down the hill. As a general rule, keep your hands on a line even with the ball. On very steep uphill lies, you might even set your hands a little behind the ball, but in no instance should you position your hands ahead of the ball; if you do, you will drive the club into the hill.

From this address position, your swing will naturally follow the slope, because your body conforms to it. This is especially important in the downswing, because then the club must move up the slope into the ball.

The club selection for uphill lies is also the direct opposite of that for downhillers. Take one more club than the distance calls for from a level lie. A shot from an uphill lie is going to go unusually high, and this reduces forward thrust. And, once again, if the entire shot is uphill, with the green above you, the *playing*

From an uphill lie, widen your stance by moving just the right foot to the right. Use a less lofted club than usual.

yardage is greater — 175 yards uphill *plays* at least 10 yards longer.

Sidehill Shots

For sidehill lies, with the ball either above or below your feet, there are no special adjustments you can make at address that will help you swing the club in conformation with the slope. However, what you must do is simple enough — just aim the club and align your body to allow for the effects on trajectory that invariably result from such lies.

When the ball is above your feet, the shot will move from right to left — a hook off a severe slope, a draw off a slight slope. With the ball below your feet, it will turn from left to right — a slice or fade, depending again on the severity of the slope.

By aiming your club and body to the right of the target when the ball is above your feet, you set up to swing back to the inside of your target line so the club will not hit the ground

AIM LEFT OF TARGET

With the ball below your feet, allow for a slice by aiming to the left of target.

behind the ball on either the takeaway or the downswing. In other words, you will naturally swing on a flatter-than-usual plane.

By aiming to the left of your target with the ball below your feet, you naturally swing the club back away from your body—outside of the target line. Again, by so doing you avoid hitting the ground behind the ball.

Never try to go "against" the terrain with these shots, because you'll be asking for trouble. For instance, if you wanted to hit a slice or fade when the ball is above your feet, then you would have to open your stance. On the backswing, you'd then take the club back to the outside—away from your body—and straight into the rising ground. To avoid hitting the hill this way, you would have to raise the club abruptly—and unnaturally. On the downswing, you would have to be a magician to make a solid contact with the ball.

The same thing happens, in reverse, if you try to hit a hook when the ball is below your feet.

What I am saying is this: If you have a shot to a pin that is on the right side of the green, but the ball is above your feet, forget about

With the ball above your feet, allow for a hook by aiming to the right of target.

going for the pin. Play for the draw or hook the lie is going to bring, hit the shot solidly, and be happy with a ball that ends up in the middle of the green, or even on the left side of it. Accept the limitations of the shot, and go for your birdies somewhere else down the line.

Club selection is the other consideration when playing sidehillers, and in one respect I go against conventional thinking on the subject.

It is true that the ball above your feet is going to produce a hook, so the ball will travel farther than usual. However, the tendency is to hit these shots too hard—for some reason, golfers feel they must *force* the shot. That is why so many golfers pull or hook these shots excessively. My advice, then, is to *use one more club* than the distance calls for—use a 5-iron where you would normally use a 6-iron—and make an *easier swing* at the ball.

When the ball is below your feet, you should also use one more club than the distance ordinarily calls for, but here the reason is that any ball that slices or fade does not carry as far as one hit straight.

AIM RIGHT OF TARGET

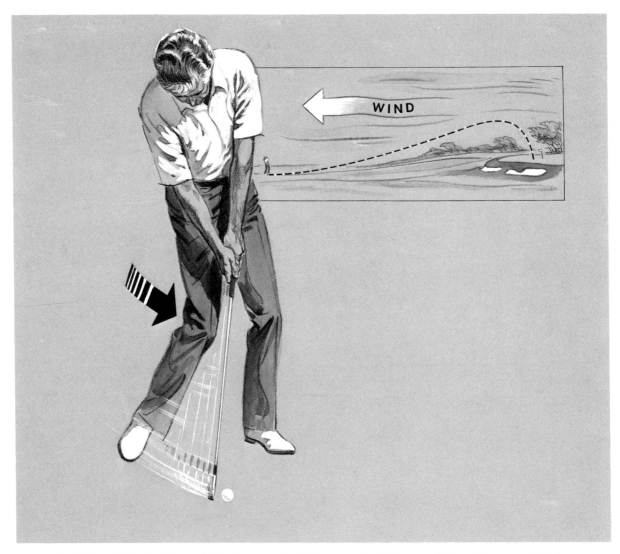

The "Riser": To play this shot, hit down on the ball and catch it higher on its back than usual. Make a strong "kick" with the right knee.

★ THE RISER

There is a situation that sometimes arises on the golf course that requires a very particular kind of shot. You have an approach *into the wind* that must carry a bunker or a water hazard in front of the green. Yet, the approach must not run beyond the putting surface because there is trouble there, too. You can't hit the standard low shot, because the ball might run over the green. A high shot is going to get caught up in the wind flutter, and fall short. If there is a bunker short of the green, the ball might "plug"—that is, bury itself in the sand.

The shot you need to hit is the "riser," in which the ball starts out low—"under" the wind—and near the end of its flight, rises well into the air so that it comes down steeply and softly to the green.

The riser is a shot for the player who can make the subtle change in his swing arc that produces the correct trajectory.

Use the club you think you need for the distance, with the wind factor included in your calculation. You must hit the ball with a more descending blow than you normally do—almost as though you were going to hit its upper half.

Widen your stance a few inches by moving *only the left foot laterally to the left*, and also set your hands slightly more to the left. With your weight a little more on the left side, and your stance widened, you can now make the more vertical, or V-shaped, swing you need. Keep your eyes on the front of the ball, rather than the back of it, to help you make contact higher up on its back than usual, and make a strong "kick" with your right knee to the left in the downswing.

To hit the riser successfully, you need the wind in your face; the shot won't come off with the wind at your back, or with no wind at all. You'll find this stroke most useful for iron-shot approaches, but you can play it with a fairway wood, provided you have a good lie. However, don't try to play the "riser" for an approach under 60 yards; at such a short distance, you can't take the aggressive swing that makes the shot work.

★ WITH THE WIND, GO LOW

When you have an approach shot in the 130-to-160-yard range with a strong wind at

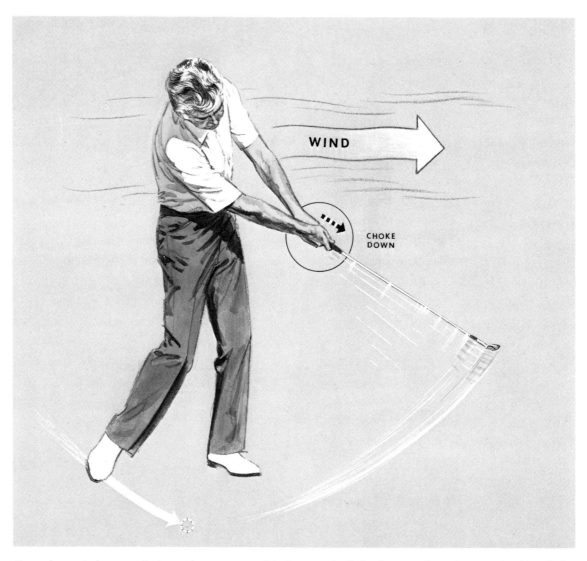

For a downwind approach shot, take one more club than usual, choke down on it, and use a "dead-handed" action. This will keep the ball "under" the wind.

your back, and plenty of level ground in front of the pin—a lot of green to "work with," as tour players say—I think it's best to hit a *low* ball.

Most golf teachers advise the opposite; they say to hit the ball high because the wind will knock it down and keep it from going too far. I don't agree. I feel that any ball hit high with a strong wind behind can't be sufficiently controlled, even by the best players. There's too much risk of the wind *not* knocking the ball down enough, or at all. I think it's better to avoid the wind as much as possible.

For this shot, use *one more club* than the distance would ordinarily require, and choke down on the grip, thereby effectively stiffening the shaft a bit, which gives you a trajectory slightly lower than normal. By choking down you also reduce the distance you'll obtain with the club—a 6-iron becomes, in effect, a 7-iron—but the stronger club's lesser loft will provide the low trajectory you're after.

In the swing, you should deaden the action of the wrists and hands as much as possible. Swing the club primarily with your arms and shoulders, making a firm weight shift to the left with the lower body in the downswing. Keeping the wrists and hands relatively inactive makes the ball fly lower, "under" the wind.

THE FLYER—HOW TO SPOT IT, HOW TO PLAY IT

A "flyer" is the result you get from certain lies in the rough or fairway. It comes off the clubface very fast, with no controlling spin, and almost always flies and rolls farther than normal.

To cope with the flyer you first must know when it will occur. There are two main types of flyer lies. One type occurs when the ball is sitting on top of wet, longish grass, with the blades lying in the direction you are playing. At impact, the blades get between the ball and the clubface and moisture forms on the surface of each, eliminating the controlling spin usually applied to the ball.

The second type of flyer lie is a little more difficult to identify. It occurs when the ball is lying atop soft grass with hard ground beneath it. The grass is not dense like U.S. Open rough, for example, from which there are few flyers. There is a lot of "air" in the grass, so there is little or no resistance to the clubhead when it strikes the ball. The clubhead over-accelerates, and you get a flyer.

You play both flyer lies in the same way—by "thinning" the ball. That is, you strike the ball a little higher on its back cover than usual. Use the same swing technique as for hitting the low ball. You also need to make a more descending blow than normal to drive the ball down.

At address, widen your stance a couple of inches by moving *only* the left foot laterally. Set your hands a bit ahead of the ball, and keep the blade square to the target line. Set the club very lightly on the top of the grass to foster the "thin" hit you want. If you were to push the club down into the grass behind the ball at address, you would tend to hit down

flush on the back of the ball, which you don't want in this case. As far as I'm concerned, you can't hit a flyer too thin.

I should point out that most flyers come from trying to "allow" for a "hotter" shot by taking, say, one less club than would normally be used for the distance. Taking less club is common advice, but I disagree with it, because you'll tend to hit too hard, and if you also hit the ball flush you'll then get a classic flyer. Just select a club which you know you can easily reach the green with, and use the techniques I've described.

The two types of "flyer" lies:
In both cases, aim to "thin" the ball a little.

★ THE SUPER-LOB

The most delicate pitch shots are those to a pin about 10 yards away, where your ball must carry over a high mound, a bunker, a water hazard, or just a stretch of very deep grass. Your ball may lie in heavy rough, on hard ground, or on nicely clipped turf.

The essential problem here is that you don't have a lot of green to work with; the pin is not very far beyond the obstacle you must carry. There is usually some green beyond the pin, but, as an advanced golfer, you want to do more than merely get the ball onto the putting surface; you want it to finish close to the hole. What you need is the super-lob with the sand wedge, a shot that hits the ball very high but with little forward flight. On landing, the ball then drops "softly" on the green with no backspin and very little roll.

The secret to making this shot lies in the length of the backswing you use. It should be *considerably longer* than you'd think.

If you were to make a short backswing to match the length of the shot we're talking about, as most golfers would do, your overall swing would be relatively quick. With a short, fast backswing, you inevitably hit the ball too hard and it goes too far for your purposes.

For the super-lob, you need *as little* clubhead speed as possible at impact. The slower the clubhead speed at this point, the more softly the ball will land. Thus, you should use a long backswing—one in which your hands reach shoulder height. This length of backswing will be much slower than a short one, because you *know* you want to hit the ball only 10 yards or so.

If the backswing is slow, it is much easier to maintain a slow pace in the downswing. In fact, the advanced golfer can even slow the downswing more, or decelerate at impact. Deceleration at impact is normally one of golf's worst sins. However, because of the length of the backswing for the super-lob, there will still be enough force at impact even with some deceleration, especially since you are using the heaviest iron club in your bag.

On the super-lob, keep the length of the backswing always the same; the length of the follow-through determines how far you hit the ball. In any case, the follow-through is normally minimal, and for the very short shots the club may not come up more than a foot off the ground after impact.

As for the setup for the shot, address the ball with an open stance, with your foot spread a little wider than usual for so short a

shot. The wider stance will prevent body movement during the swing. Play the ball where you normally do – left of center.

Aim the *blade squarely at the target*; this means it will be *open* in relation to your body, which is aligned to the left of the target. Do not open the clubface to where it's aimed to the right of the target, or you will put too much "bounce" on the sand wedge. This will lead to thinned or "bladed" shots when playing from hard ground.

I recommend a "weak" left-hand grip for the super-lob – the hand turned to the left so the V formed by the thumb and index finger points to your left shoulder. The "weak" left hand helps to "deaden" the shot so that it will roll less after landing.

Unlike your practice when making other short shots, *do not choke down* on the club. Hold it at the end of the handle, which will make it easier for you to make a long backswing.

Finally, use a light grip pressure, so light that someone could pull the club out of your hands with an easy tug. This also will help you make the slow backswing you need.

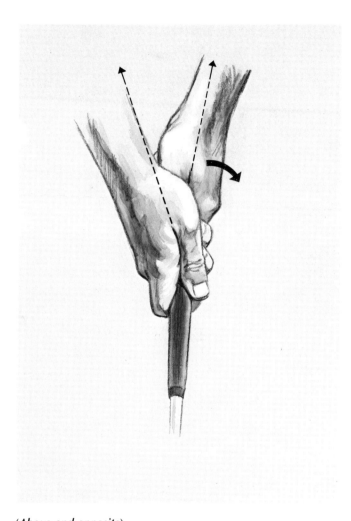

(*Above and opposite*)
The "Super-Lob": Adopt a "weak" left hand grip, with a normal right hand grip. Set up with an open stance with the blade aimed squarely at the target. Then use an extra-long, slow swing.

★ NO-BOUNCE "SAND-CLIP" BUNKER SHOTS

What made the sand wedge so popular when it was first introduced in the 1930s was how much easier it made getting out of the sand. The key was the "bounce" built into the sole. I have explained "bounce" earlier, in the section on the pitch shot, but will review it again here briefly.

A sand wedge has bounce if the back edge of its sole is lower than the leading edge when the club is set on the ground in the address position. Because the back edge is lowest, it strikes the sand first — before the leading edge. This prevents the wedge from digging down too deeply, which was the main problem with the niblick (9-iron) that had been used before. So, ever since the invention of the sand wedge, instruction on how to play from bunkers has included the phrase "Hit about 2 inches behind the ball."

That is still good advice for the average golfer, who needs that margin for error. But I believe the advanced player does not, that he has the skill to play a "no-bounce" wedge and thereby greatly increase his control over the shot.

The sand wedge with bounce demands an explosion: The ball flies out of the trap in a mass of sand. Because the clubface never touches the ball, you apply very little backspin, and the ball will have a fair amount of run after landing. It is always difficult to judge just how much run there will be. That, of course, is the least of the average golfer's worries — he just wants to get the ball somewhere on the green. However, the advanced golfer is *sure* he can get out of a bunker, so he wants a more precise shot. He can get that with a no-bounce wedge.

(Note: All mass-produced sand wedges are made with bounce, so to get one without it you will have to make a special order. Alternatively, have a good club repairman grind the bounce off your present sand wedge.)

"Clip" the Ball

On a regular iron shot played from the grass, the clubhead hits the ball *and* the ground on which it is sitting at the same time. The sand shot with the no-bounce wedge comes very, very close to that type of impact, hitting the sand just barely behind the ball, then going under it and taking a shallow divot. The ball is

The "Clip" shot from a greenside bunker: Put an imaginary tee beneath the ball, and just graze the top of the tee as you clip the ball out of the sand.

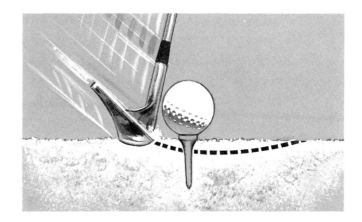

not exploded out, but rather, as I like to put it, "clipped" out of the sand. Because so much less sand gets between the clubface and the ball at impact than with an explosion, you do impart backspin to the ball.

Basic Method...with a Difference

The basic mechanics for playing the "sand clip" shot are no different than for playing the explosion. I outlined these in full earlier, so I'll only restate essentials here.

Take an open stance, and spread your feet extra wide to prevent body movement during the swing. Distribute your weight evenly and play the ball in your standard position, some-

where left of center. Aim the clubface *squarely at the target.* Swing the club back and through primarily with the hands, arms, and shoulders.

The difference with the clip shot is that at impact, the club is very close to the ball, which takes the kind of refined clubhead control an advanced golfer has.

My favorite illustration of what I mean by a clip shot is the same one I described, briefly, for the basic greenside bunker shot—but with a slight difference with the advanced golfer in mind. Push a tee into the sand and place a ball on it so it is sitting on the very surface of the sand—a perfect lie. I suggested that in playing the shot, the average golfer should try to split the tee in half. The advanced player should be a little finer, just grazing the top of the tee as he clips the ball.

Do not think about hitting the ball, but just the top of the tee beneath it. In fact, I look at the top center of the ball during the stroke, in a sense "seeing" the tee underneath.

Not only do you get a lot of backspin with the "clip shot," you have great control over the distance you hit the ball, because, again, your impact point is so close to it. You can apply the same sense of touch for distance as on chip shots and pitches from grass.

KEN VENTURI won the 1964 U.S. Open with one of the most dramatic finishes in the history of that or any other championship as he came near to collapsing from heat exhaustion. This victory at Washington, D.C.'s Congressional Golf Club capped Venturi's playing career. Soon after, a hand ailment sent Venturi into early retirement from competitive golf at the age of thirty-three. But between 1957 and 1967 he won ten professional tournaments, was the 1964 PGA Player-of-the-Year, and a member of the 1965 U.S. Ryder Cup team.

Since then, Venturi has established himself as an exceptionally astute student of golf technique. He is a "pro's pro," one of those few to whom the touring professionals go when they need help with their games. But Venturi also reaches the average golfer through his many clinics, and as golf analyst on the CBS network's golf telecasts.

A native of San Francisco, Venturi presently is golf director at the Eagle Creek Golf and Tennis Club, in Naples, Florida, where he resides.

AL BARKOW was chief writer for "Shell's Wonderful World of Golf" television series, and is now editor-in-chief of *Golf Illustrated*. His other books include *Golf's Golden Grind, the History of the Tour*; *The Good Sense of Golf*, with Billy Casper; *The Venturi Analysis*, with Ken Venturi; *The Art of Putting*, with George Low; and *Gettin' To The Dance Floor*, which won the 1986 United States Golf Association International Book Award. A fine amateur golfer who has competed at national level, Barkow lives in Woodside, New York.